SAND GULL

Poems of Du Fu

Volume 3

Translated by
Kwan-Hung Chan

SAND GULL

沙

鷗

Contents

Year 757   29

Year 758.. 51

Year 759.. 53

Year 760-764   69

Year 768-770 252

POEMS NOT IN CHRONOLOGY 271

PREFACE

Du Fu (712-770) 杜甫 is known among the Chinese as a poet with the genius of a sage, on the same platform with Li Bai (701-762) 李白 with the genius of an immortal, Bai Juyi (772-842) 白居易 with the genius of a mortal and Li He (790-816) 李賀 with the genius of a ghost.

Eleven years younger than Li Bai, Du Fu looked up to him as a friend and poet and wrote quite a few poems in his praise. The affinity between them was mutual. After death, both have been critiqued by their supporters and detractors, with the aim to determine supremacy. Through the centuries, comparative studies on their poetic achievements have been legion but largely inconclusive.

A more productive attempt would be to examine the similar terms and phrases used by Chinese ancient poets to gain a better understanding of poetry in general and

1

translation in particular. At least, two expressions are worth our attention.

The first expression is 無情. In most cases, it can be interpreted and translated as "heartless" or "callous". The well-known poem "Given in Farewell" 贈別 by Du Mu (803-852) 杜牧 begins with these two lines: 多情卻似總無情，唯覺樽前笑不成 which can be translated as "She is amorous, yet seems callous in the main. Just a smile over our farewell drink she cannot feign." 多情 "amorous" and 無情 "callous" have opposite meanings.

The same expression was used by Li Bai in his poem "Drinking Alone under the Moon" 月下獨酌。 After describing his pleasure of drinking under moonlight, he concluded with his wish for a future reunion with the moon. 永結無情遊， 相期邈雲漢 "Forever bonded and fully engaged in play, I hope for a reunion on the far Milky Way." The poet looked forward to a whole-hearted reunion with the moon, making a heartless get-together illogical.

In a lesser-known poem of Du Fu, "Five Songs by the River: Gardenias" 江頭五詠：梔子, the expression 無情 also appeared. Much attracted by the gardenias by the river, he wrote in conclusion 無情移得汝，貴在映江波 "With boundless zest, I transplanted you. Against river waves, rare is your reflection in view." It would be irrational to think De Fu transplanted the gardenias heartlessly.

These poems point to the fact that in Chinese classical poetry, 無情 can mean 盡情, depending on the context. It should be noted that when Chinese intellectuals translate Li Bai's poem "Drinking under the Moon" from the classical literary language 文言 to the colloquial language 白話, this semantic flexibility is followed.

The second expression is 床, commonly known as "bed". In the famous poem of Li Bai "Thoughts in the Quiet Night" 靜夜思, the first two lines 床前明月光， 疑是地上霜 are often translated as "Before my bed is bright moonlight, Taken for the frost on the ground." Because a bedroom scene indoors is followed by a frosty ground outdoors, some doubt if the poet was really referring to a sleeping bed.

In Tang poetry, the term 床 is frequently linked with 井. For example, Li Bai wrote 梧桐落金井, 一葉飛銀床. Similarly, Du Fu created these images 風箏吹玉柱, 露井凍銀床. Both 井 and 床 are outdoor objects close together.

The most significant clue may be gleaned from the poem of Li He written in 814: "A Dug Well in the Backyard" 後園鑿井歌, with these beginning lines 井上轆轤床上轉, 水聲緊, 弦聲淺, translated as "On a framed axis, the pulley above a well turns. Loudly the water flows. Quietly the rope goes." This poem depicts 床 as a framed structure associated with the pulley 轆轤 above a well 井.

Already in the 760's, Du Fu mentioned 轆轤 in close association with 井. In his poem "on the New Study Hall at the Confucius Temple of Mount Heng County, Shown to Magistrate

Lu" 題衡山縣文宣王廟新學堂呈陸宰, he wrote "In torrid summer, there is a well, with a pulley to get water to chill a stairway." 有井朱夏時，轆轤凍階阤.

These poems substantiate the claim that in the poem "Thoughts in the Quiet Night", Li Bai was not looking at a sleeping bed but the frame for the pulley above a well, with the moonlit ground in front.

In the study of the two expressions chosen, examples of usage by poets come from verses in "Three Hundred Tang Poems" and also those excluded by the compilers of this classic, especially in the case of Li He. For a comprehensive analysis of the linguistic and prosodic characteristics of Chinese classical poetry, our sources of reference should be as broad-based as possible.

Not used to the culture and climate of the areas south of Changan, Du Fu planned to go home. In Kuizhou, he asked a friend to take a letter to seek out his old estate in Tulou near Luoyang. Then he had a boat built for a long trip back home.

In 768, Du Fu set out with his family and a servant to Luoyang, with side trips to visit friends and relatives on his voyage. This long-term leisurely activity suggests that he had savings after gainful employments in the previous years.

When ill health caught up with him, Du Fu died on the boat in Tanzhou in 770, with much regret. The poems written around this time reveal his memorable activities in reunions and new ventures. He died while doing things he always wanted to do.

256 poems are included in this volume. I have grouped some later poems of Du Fu under several broad periods of time: 760-764 Chengdu Years, 765-767 Kuizhou Years and 768-770 Voyage Home. Other poems on nature or non-specific events are listed under "Poems Not in Chronology", in alphabetical order by title. In a few cases, the archaic Chinese characters used are replaced by their modern and variant forms. Friends and relatives have helped me in completing this volume and I would like to thank them for their support.

1:

POEMS IN CHRONOLOGY

****

Year 746

飲中八仙歌

知章騎馬似乘船，眼花落井水底眠。

汝陽三斗始朝天，道逢麴車口流涎，恨不移封向酒泉。

左相日興費萬錢，飲如長鯨吸百川，銜杯樂聖稱避賢。

宗之瀟灑美少年，舉觴白眼望青天，皎如
玉樹臨風前

蘇晉長齋繡佛前，醉中往往愛逃禪。

李白一斗詩百篇，長安市上酒家眠。天子
呼來不上船， 自稱臣是酒中仙。

張旭三杯草聖傳。脫帽露頂王公前，揮毫
落紙如雲煙

焦遂五斗方卓然，高談雄辯驚四筵。

Eight Immortals of the Wine Cup

A boatman riding a horse, Zhizhang
    seems to be.
He falls in a well and sleeps under water,
    looking dizzy.

To see the king, the Prince of Ruyang
    needs three quarts of wine to get
    ready.
Meeting a brewer's cart on the road,
    he drools already.
His zest to move his fiefdom to Wine
    Spring is of the highest degree.

Each day, the Chancellor spends a fortune
  and feels happy.
He drinks like a long whale, draining
  a hundred streams with his energy.
He likes good, clear ale, called
  "Holy" and shuns thick ones, called
  "Worthy"

A dashing and handsome lad is Cui
  Zhongzhi.
He raises his cup and with disdain,
  looks skyward at infinity,
Before the wind, like a white jade tree.

In front of an embroidered image of
  Buddha,
Sui Jin vows to abstain constantly
Drunk, from the restrictions of Chan
  Buddhism, he wants to be free.

Li Bai writes a hundred poems, after
  one quart of wine merely.
He sleeps in a tavern of Changan City.
When summoned by the king to his
  boat, he wants to flee,
Declaring, "I am an immortal when
  tipsy."

Zhang Xu is known as "Draft Script
   Sage" when drunk only.
With his cap off, he writes with his
   hair for princes and nobles to see.
Like cloud and mist, the brush strokes
   on paper move with subtlety.

That Jiao Sui excels after three quarts
   of wine, we agree.
At feasts, he shocks all in pushing a
   case or making a plea.

Year 751

前出塞九首， 其一

戚戚去故里， 悠悠赴交河。 公家有程期，
亡命嬰禍羅。 君已富土境， 開邊一何多。
棄絕父母恩， 吞聲行負戈。

Crossing the Passes, First Series,
No. 1

In low spirits, I leave my hometown,
For distant Jiaohe, on my way.
Our government has set schedules.

For a deserter's crime, his family has to pay.
The king has already owned a vast territory.
Why does he need frontier land far away?
I swallow my sobs, carry my arms and march.
My parent's kindness is something I can never repay.

前出塞九首， 其二

出門日已遠，不受徒旅欺。骨肉恩豈斷，
男兒死無時。走馬脫彎頭，手中挑青絲。
捷下萬仞崗，俯身試搴旗。

Crossing the Passes, First Series, No.2

I have not been harassed in traveling on the march.
From my home, daily it is further away.
Of course, my love for my flesh and blood is unbroken.
A man can die any day.
I gallop with the bridle off.

With a blue silk cord in hand, I play.
I stop and try to snatch up a banner,
After coming down a ridge of great
  height with no delay.

前出塞九首，　其三

磨刀嗚咽水，水赤刃傷手。欲輕腸斷聲，
心緒亂已久。丈夫誓許國，憤惋復何有。
功名圖麒麟，戰骨當速朽。

Crossing the Passes, First Series, No. 3

The water turns red when the blade cuts
  my hand.
I sharpen my sword with the water
  sobbing for me.
I try to ignore the heart-breaking sound,
But for a long time, from stress my
  disturbed mind is not free.
Where is room for anger and regret
When a man swears on his life for his
  country?
One may be honored with a portrait in
  the Unicorn Pavilion,

But in rapid decay, the bones of the war
  dead will be.

前出塞九首，　其四

送徒既有長，遠戍亦有身。生死向前去，
不勞吏怒瞋。路逢相識人，附書與六親。
哀哉兩卻絕，不復同苦辛。

Crossing the Passes, First Series, No.4

A captain takes drafted soldiers to the front.
There are body counts at garrisons for
  warfare.
We march forward, life or death.
There is no need for the army recruiter's
  angry stare.
I met on the road someone I know
And sent to my kin a letter in his care.
Sadly, we are kept apart.
Of hardships at home, I shall not again
  get a share.

前出塞九首，其五

迢迢萬里餘，領我赴三軍。軍中異苦樂，
主將寧盡聞。隔河見胡騎，倏忽數百群。
我始為奴僕，幾時樹功勛。

Crossing the Passes, First Series, No.5

We were led to the Main Armed Forces,
More than ten thousand miles away.
Experiences of hardship and joy differ in
    the army.
Information for the commander is not in
    full relay.
Across the river, I see nomad cavalries,
That gather in hundreds, without delay.
I start my duty as a slave and servant.
To reap awards for success, when is the
    day?

前出塞九首，其六

挽弓當挽強，用箭當用長。射人先射馬，
擒賊先擒王。殺人亦有限，列國自有疆。
苟能制侵陵，豈在多殺傷。

Crossing the Passes, First Series, No.6

To pull bows, pull ones that are strong.
To use arrows, use ones that are long.
To shoot a man, first shoot his horse.
To capture foes, capture their chief first
   and headlong.
There are limits to killing.
States have their borders all along.
There would not be full-scale casualties
If only invasions could be curbed by the
   sense of right or wrong.

前出塞九首， 其七

驅馬天欲雪， 軍行入高山。 徑危抱寒石，
指落曾冰間。 已去漢月遠， 何時築城還。
浮雲暮南征， 可望不可攀。

Crossing the Passes, First Series, No.7

The sky is about to snow as we gallop.
The army is marching into the hills at a
   height.
Our fingers slip into icy piles.

15

On a steep trail, we cling to cold rocks tight.
When shall we return after building a wall,
Already far from my hometown's moonlight?
We are unable to climb to some visible
  floating clouds
That head south at twilight.

前出塞九首，　其八

單于寇我壘，百里風塵昏。雄劍四五動，
彼軍為我奔。虜其明王歸，繫頸授轅門。
潛身備行列，一勝何足倫。

Crossing the Passes, First Series, No.8

The chieftain of the Huns raided our fort.
The dust storms of war for endless miles
  cast a shadow.
Their army flees before us
As a few strokes of our swords in heroism
  go.
The prisoner, with a cord around his neck
  at the Commander's gate,
Is the captured chieftain that we know.
What is the worth discussing one victory

When among the ranks, my status is low?

前出塞九首，　其九

從軍十年餘，能無分寸功。衆人貴苟得，
欲語羞雷同。中原有鬥爭，況在狄與戎。
丈夫四海志，安可辭固窮。

Crossing the Passes, First Series, No.9

I have been with the army for more than
　ten years.
Can I not achieve something, however
　slight?
Most people value any gain by chance.
I feel shamed speaking for a similar insight.
Wars are going on in the Central Plains,
More with the Di and Rong tribes, engaged
　in fight.
A man's ambition rests with the Four Seas.
How can I refuse to have my loyalty
　held tight?

Year 753

白絲行

繰絲須長不須白，越羅蜀錦金粟尺。象床
玉手亂殷紅，萬草千花動凝碧。已悲素質
隨時染，裂下鳴機色相對。美人細意熨帖
平，裁縫減盡針線跡。春天衣著為君舞，
蛺蝶飛來黃鸝語。落絮遊絲亦有情，隨風
照日宜輕舉。香汗輕塵汙顏色，開新合故
置何許。君不見才士汲引難，恐懼棄捐人
羈旅。

Ballad of White Silk

Silk-reeling needs long threads that may
    not be white,
To make Yue gauze and Shu brocade,
    using a yardstick with gold inlay.
Countless blooms and herbs come alive
    with a still backdrop of green.
On an ivory frame, jade-like hands weave
    dark red reels in disarray.
I am already sad over some white silk
    being dyed any time.
Like split silk, the creaking loom moves

dyed strands in a spray.
A beauty carefully irons it flat,
Tailoring to hide needlework all the way.
It is a robe worn to dance for a man.
As butterflies flit, orioles trill on a spring
    day.
Wind-borne and sunlit things should rise
    lightly.
To our emotion, falling fluff and gossamer
    play.
Fragrant sweat and light dust soil the colors.
Where do we place newly opened pieces
    and have old ones put away?
Do you not see, it is hard to recruit talented
    people
Who, fearing abandonment, as detained
    wanderers, bear with their stay.

Year 754

渼陂行

岑參兄弟皆好奇，攜我遠來遊渼陂。天地
黤慘忽異色，波濤萬頃堆琉璃。琉璃汗漫
泛舟入，事殊興極憂思集。鼉作鯨吞不復

19

知，惡風白浪何嗟及。主人錦帆相為開，舟子喜甚無氛埃。鳧鷖散亂棹謳發，絲管啁啾空翠來。沉竿續蔓深莫測，菱葉荷花靜如拭。宛在中流渤澥清，下歸無極終南黑。半陂已南純浸山，動影裊窕沖融間。船舷暝戛雲際寺，水面月出藍田關。此時驪龍亦吐珠，馮夷擊鼓群龍趨。湘妃漢女出歌舞，金支翠旗光有無。咫尺但愁雷雨至，蒼茫不曉神靈意。少壯幾時奈老何，向來哀樂何其多。

Ballad of Lake Meipi

Cen Shen and his brother like wonders in
  nature, I say.
They brought me for a boat ride on Lake
  Meipi far away.
Suddenly, the bluish black earth and sky
  have changed colors.
In piles of lapis, gigantic billows make
  an array.

With lapis-like waves all over, on a boat
  we go.
Most elated at the special event, I let my
  anxiety show.
About being preys of alligators and whales,

20

I do not know.
Let alone many a menacing gust and white
   billow.

The hosts' brocade sails are up and in gear.
Boatmen are much pleased with the air,
   dust-free and clear.
Wild ducks and seagulls scatter as
   fishermen's songs begin.
Short notes from pipes and strings from a
   sunlit sky, I can hear.

Poles and cords cannot fathom the depth
   of the waters.
Still water caltrops leaves and lotus blooms
   are spotless.
We seem to be in the limpid midstream of
   a gulf of the Yellow River
Which engulfs the infinite, black shadow
   of Mount Zhongnan no less.

The lake's southern half holds the
   reflected hill in its entrance.
From the depth, the shadow shows its
   unsettling face.
The side of our boat touches a temple by
   the clouds.
From Lantian Pass, there is moonrise on

the water's surface.

Now like Black Dragon spitting pearls,
    the sky shows starlight.
Dragons follow Water Fairy's drumbeats
    keenly in flight.
Xiang goddesses and Han maidens sing
    and dance.
Golden poles and kingfisher banners come
    in and out of sight.

I worry about a thunderstorm getting close
And know not, in the boundless void, how
    Heaven's will goes.
Can we stop aging and let youth last?
Often joy turns into grief, now as in the past.

與鄠縣源大少府宴渼陂（得寒字）

應為西陂好，金錢罄一餐。飯炒雲子白，
瓜嚼水精寒。無計囘船下，空愁避酒難。
主人情爛熳，持答翠琅玕。

Feasting at Meipi with District Defender of Hu County, Yuan Senior (My Allotted Rhyme is "Cold")

It must be due to fine West Lake Meipi
That on a meal, you use up your gold.
We shovel white rice, like cloud fragments,
  into our mouths,
Chewing melons, crystalline and cold.
I worry for dodging wine is hard.
A plan to return to my boat, I do not hold.
Let me use this to answer your rare poem,
  like a gemstone.
The host is exceptional in kindness, with
  nothing to withhold.

投贈哥舒開府翰十二韻

I

近代麒麟閣，何人第一功？君王自神武，
駕馭必英雄。開府當朝傑，論兵邁古風。
先鋒百戰在，略地兩隅空。青海無傳箭，
天山早掛弓。廉頗仍走敵，魏絳已和戎。
每惜河湟棄，新兼節制通。智謀垂睿想，

23

出入冠諸公。日月低秦樹，乾坤繞漢宮。
胡人愁逐北，宛馬又從東。

II

受命邊沙遠，歸來禦席同。軒墀曾寵鶴，
畋獵舊非熊。茅土加名數。山河誓始終。
策行遺戰伐，契合動昭融。勳業青冥上，
交親氣概中。未為珠履客，已見白頭翁。
壯節初題柱，生涯獨轉蓬。幾年春草歇，
今日暮途窮。軍事留孫楚，行間識呂蒙。
防身一長劍，將欲倚崆峒。

For Geshu Han, Supreme Commandant, in Twenty Couplets

In the Hall of Fame of this age,
To whom does the top honor go?
Our king with his divine might,
Must have recruited many a hero.

Your war strategy beats ancient styles.
The supreme commander is a hero of the
    palace.
After a hundred battles, our vanguard
    general persists.
Full control of two regions is in place.

Battles ended in Kokonor.
From wars, Tianshan has been free.
Like Wei Jiang, you have made peace with
    the nomads.
Like Lian Po, you can still rid your enemy.

The defeat near Yellow River and Huang
    River is your regret.
Though as the military commander,
    recovery was newly done.
The king thinks highly of your wise plans.
Everywhere, your fame tops everyone.

The sun and moon at a height shine on trees
    of the capital.
Our palace stands with Heaven and Earth
    all around.
Foreign rebels rush back north in sorrow.
Again, Ferghana horses as tributes are
    eastward bound.

II

You feast with the king on return,
After expeditions to the deserts far away.
Like cranes as pets, rebels were once
    favored.
Through luck, our state got your help in

a grand way.

You were enfeoffed with land and title
Which will forever remain.
Your plan and action will end all wars.
Good bonding brings about a brilliant reign.

The value of your contribution is sky-high.
With friendliness, you show your care.
I have not met a benefactor,
Already with a head of white hair.

My life is now like that of a tumbleweed.
With a strong will, I first entered society
    on a former day.
Spring grass has had several yearly cycles.
I am at the roadblock of my life today.

You retain military experts in your
    headquarters.
Among the ranks, you recognize and
    promote the best.
I have a long sword for self-protection.
To rest it by a mountain like you, let my
    wish be expressed.

渼陂西南台

高臺面蒼陂，　六月風日冷。　蒹葭離披去，
天水相與永。　懷新目似擊，　接要心已領。
仿像識鮫人，　空濛辨魚艇。　錯磨終南翠，
顛倒白閣影。　嶄崒增光輝，　乘陵惜俄頃。
勞生愧嚴鄭，　外物慕張邴。　世復輕驊騮，
吾甘雜蛙黽。　知歸俗可忽，　取適事莫并，
身退豈待官，　老來苦便靜。　洗資菱芡足，
庶結茅茨舟，　彌年逐清景。

The Terrace Southwest of Lake Meipi

The high terrace faces a deep blue lake.
It is a cold windy day in July.
Reeds and rushes have waned and gone.
The horizon is forever seamless at the
　　verge of the sky.

My mind is already receptive to the
　　essences of life.
To my eyes, striking are things that are new.
I make out the vague resemblance of mermen.
In the mist and rain, with fishing boats barely
　　in view.

Waves hone the reflected verdant Mount

Zhongnan.
Lofty peaks get extra bright.
The image of White Pavilion in water is
    upside down.
Time is too short for me to scale the
    height.

Belabored by life, I feel shame before
    recluses: Yan and Zheng.
I admire hermits: Zhang and Bing, for
    shunning material things.
I am happy to be among commoners,
    like frogs.
Like rare horses, geniuses are bypassed
    by worldlings.

The custom of returning home can be
    overlooked.
Instead of doing last-ditch fights, I
    choose to do what I please.
Why wait to be an office-bearer to resign
    from public life.
Old, I work hard to seek quietude and ease.

With enough water caltrops and chicken
    heads,
I shall build a thatched hut on a remote lot.
From now on, in a small boat,

Year in year out, I shall pursue the scenery
of any secluded spot.

Year 757

徒步歸行

明公壯年值時危，經濟實籍英雄姿。國之
社稷今若是，武定禍亂非公誰。鳳翔千官
且飽飯，衣馬不復能輕肥。青袍朝士最困
者，白頭拾遺徒步歸。

人生交契無老少，論交何必先同調。妻子
山中哭向天，須公櫪上追風驃。

Ballad of Returning Home on Foot

Your Highness meets the current national
crisis in your prime.
Your heroism is your mainstay.
If the country's institutions can run as
done today,
Who but you could have ended riots by
force in time?

Countless officials at Fengxiang have rice
    in good supply,
But no more in white silk robes can they
    ride well-fed horses.
Of the low-ranking courtiers, the one in
    most hardship
Is this white-haired reminder going home
    on foot.

In life, regardless of age, to make friends
    one can try.
On like minds, friendship should not rely.
I need a wind-chasing steed from your
    stables.
In the mountain, facing Heaven, my wife
    and children cry.

大雲寺贊公房四首，其一

心在水精域，衣霑春雨時。洞門盡徐步，
深院果幽期。到扉開復閉，撞鐘齋及茲。
醍醐長發性，飲食過扶衰。把臂有多日，
開懷無愧辭。黃鸝度結構，紫鴿下罘罳。
愚意會所適，花邊行自遲。湯休起我病，
微笑索題時。

The Chamber of Monk Zan in Great Clouds Temple, no.1

My mind is with the Crystal Palace.
My robe is wet with spring rain.
I walk slowly through all gates,
For the deep courtyard, with quietude to
    gain.
The struck bell tells mealtime is now.
I open a door and close it again.
Like cream, Buddhist wisdom is refined.
Food and drink here perk my health on
    the wane.
For days we move about arm in arm,
Open-hearted, with a common language,
    simple and plain.
A purple dove descends to nets and traps.
I follow what suits me.
By flowers, a slow walk I maintain.
A poem is solicited with a smile.
Tang Huixiu will let my health regain.

大雲寺贊公房四首，其二

細軟青絲履，光明白氈巾。深藏供老宿，
取用及吾身。自顧轉無趣，交情何尚新。

道林方不世，惠遠德過人。雨瀉暮簷竹，
風吹春井芹。天陰對圖畫，最覺潤龍麟。

The Chamber of Monk Zan in Great Clouds Temple, no.2

Soft slippers in fine green silk
And shining cotton kerchiefs in white
Are kept well for old resident monks.
To use them, I am given the right.
Why is our friendship still fresh?
In retrospect, I lack interesting insight.
Huiyuan's virtues surpassed others.
Daolin's talent was bypassed from
   oversight.
Celeries near a well gets wind blown.
Rain pours on bamboos by the eaves at
   twilight.
I sense most the moisture on dragon scales
When I look at a painting under weak
   sunlight.

大雲寺贊公房四首，其三

燈影照無睡，心清聞妙香。夜深殿突兀，
風動金琅璫。天黑閉春院，地清棲暗芳。

玉繩迴斷絕，鐵鳳森翱翔。梵放時出寺，
鐘殘仍殷床。明朝在沃野，苦見塵沙黃。

The Chamber of Monk Zan in Great Clouds Temple, no 3

With a clear mind, I smell the fragrant
    incense,
Sleepless under lamplight.
Ding Dong goes the copper wind chime.
The hall towers over me, deep in the night.
On this open land, scented blooms lie hidden.
In spring, the courtyard is shut at twilight.
The constellation, Jade Rope, winds and
    breaks.
Iron phoenixes in the dark soar in flight.
Sanskrit chants at times come from the
    temple.
Trailing bell chimes still shake my bed,
    though slight.
Near dawn, I shall be in the fertile wilds
Where yellow dust is a stressful sight.

大雲寺贊公房四首，其四

童兒汲井華，慣捷品上手。沾灑不濡地，
掃除似無帚。明霞爛複閣，霽霧搴高牖。
側塞破徑花，飄颻委墀柳。艱難世事迫，
隱遁佳期後。晤語契深心，那能總鉗口。
奉辭還杖策，暫別終回首。泱泱泥汙人，
狺狺國多狗。既未免羈絆，時來憩奔走。
近公如白雪，執熱煩何有。

The Chamber of Monk Zan in Great Clouds Temple, no. 4

A lad draws the well's frothy water with
   a pitcher
And handles it nimbly in his usual way.
He sweeps as if not using a broom
And without making the ground too wet,
   shoots a spray.

Bright clouds make layered pavilions glow.
Lifting fog pulls up high windows.
Flowers blanket paths in full.
Wind sways courtyard willows.

I am hard pressed by life
And have to put retirement in seclusion

in delay.
Through talks face to face, our hearts are
    deeply bonded.
How can one always claim there is
    nothing to say?

I take my leave, holding a cane.
As we part, I turn my head.
Like huge mud, slanderers can smear
    people.
Like barking dogs, rebels in the capital
    are widespread.

Entanglements of life are still with me.
In time, from running around I may rest.
You remind me of white snow as I get
    near you.
By troubles like holding something hot,
    how can I be stressed?

月

天上秋期近，人間月影清。入河蟾不沒，
搗藥兔長生。只益丹心苦，能添白髮明。
干戈知滿地，休照國西營。

Moon

As autumn draws near in the sky,
On earth, moonlight is clear.
The Toad does not drown in the Milky Way.
The Hare pounds its herbs and live from
    year to year.
My loyal heart gets more bitter.
I have got more white hair.
Do not shine on the homesick soldiers in
    camps of the west capital
Since we know warfare is everywhere.

北鄰

明府豈辭滿，藏身方告勞。青錢買野竹，
白幘岸江臯。愛酒晉山簡，能詩何水曹。
時來訪老疾，步屟到蓬萊。

My Neighbor to the North

His Honor did not wait until his term
    expired.
Hiding, he said work had worn him down.
He bought wild bamboos with green coins.
Wearing his white headdress, he stays
    by the river's swampy shore.

Like Shan Jian of Jin, he loves wine.
His poems resemble those of He Xun of
  the Waterways Section years before.
At times, he visits this sick old man,
Strolling over to my hut among weeds,
  out of town.

北征

I

黃帝二載秋，閏八月初吉。杜子將北征，
蒼茫問家室。維時遭艱虞，朝野少暇日。
顧慚恩私被，詔許歸蓬蓽。拜辭詣闕下，
怵惕久未出。雖乏諫諍姿，恐君有遺失。
君誠中興主，經緯固密勿。東朝反未已，
臣甫憤所切。揮淚戀所在，道途猶恍惚。
乾坤含瘡痍，憂虞何時畢？

II

靡靡踰阡陌。人煙眇蕭瑟。所遇多被傷，
呻吟更流血。回首鳳翔縣，旌旗晚明滅。
前登寒山重，屢得飲馬窟。邠郊入地底，
涇水中蕩潏。猛虎立我前，蒼崖吼時裂。

37

菊垂今秋花，石戴古車轍。青雲動高興，
幽事亦客悅。山果多瑣細，羅生雜橡栗。
或紅如丹砂，或黑如點漆。雨露之所濡，
甘苦齊結實。緬思桃源內，益嘆身世拙。
陂陀望鄜時，巖谷互出沒。我行已水濱，
我僕猶木末。鴟鳥鳴黃桑，野鼠拱亂穴。
夜深經戰場，寒月照白骨。潼關百萬師，
往者散何卒！遂令半秦民，殘害為異物。

III

況我墮胡塵，及歸盡華髮。經年至茅屋，
妻子衣百結。慟哭松聲廻，悲泉共幽咽。
平生所嬌兒，顏色白勝雪。見耶背面啼，
垢膩腳不襪。床前兩小女，補綻才過膝。
海圖坼波濤，舊繡移曲折。天吳及紫鳳，
顛倒在短褐。老夫情懷惡，嘔泄臥數日。
那無囊中帛，救汝寒凜慄。粉黛亦解包，
衾裯稍羅列。瘦妻面復光，癡女頭自櫛。
學母莫不為，曉妝隨手抹。移時施朱鉛，
狼籍畫眉闊。生還對童稚，似欲忘飢渴。
問事競挽鬚，誰能即嗔喝。翻思在賊愁，
甘受雜亂聒。新歸且慰意，生理焉得說。

IV

至尊尚蒙塵，幾日休練卒。仰觀天色改，
坐覺妖氛豁。陰風西北來，慘澹隨回紇。
其王願助順，其俗善馳突。送兵五千人，
驅馬一萬匹。此輩少為貴，四方服勇決。
所用皆鷹騰，破敵過箭疾。聖心頗虛佇，
時議氣欲奪。伊洛指掌收，西京不足拔。
官軍請深入，蓄銳可俱發。此舉開青徐，
旋瞻略恆碣。昊天積霜露，正氣有肅殺。
禍轉亡胡歲。勢成擒胡月。胡命其能久，
皇綱未宜絕。

V

憶昨狼狽初，事與古先別。姦臣竟葅醢，
同惡隨蕩析。不聞夏殷衰，中自誅褒妲。
周漢獲再興，宣光果明哲。桓桓陳將軍，
仗鉞奮忠烈。微爾人盡非，於今國猶活。
淒涼大同殿，寂寞白獸闥。都人望翠華，
佳氣向金闕。園陵固有神，掃灑數不缺。
煌煌太宗業，樹立甚宏達。

My Northern Journey

On the first day of the intercalary eighth

month,
In fall of the second year of our king's reign,
I, Du Fu, was about to go north,
To see my family over a boundless terrain.

It is a period of hardship for our country.
For all, few days are leisurely and free.
I reflected on my undeserved favor from
  the king
Who let me return to my humble hut with
  his decree.

At the palace, I bowed to the king before
  leaving.
Long I lingered, with caution and fright.
Though not a competent reminder,
I still worry about his oversight.

A true leader in national revival,
He rules with diligence and care.
I am very angry over eastern barbarians,
For we are still in warfare.

In tears, I made myself leave the palace
And felt absent-minded on the way.
Everywhere there is suffering.
To end our worries, when is the day?

II

Slowly, I dragged myself across the land,
Scarcely populated and desolate.
Those I met we groaning and bleeding,
Almost in the same wounded state.

I looked back at Fengxiang County
With faded banners, in and out of sight.
Then in the cold, I climbed layered hills.
Water-holes for horses were oft in sight.

On the low land of the Binzhou outskirts,
In its midst, waters of River Jing flow.
A fierce tiger stood roaring before me.
Gray cliffs could crack at the echo.

Chrysanthemums of this fall bloomed.
Ruts of ancient carts showed on stone.
My spirit was roused as I reached the
    clouds' height.
Happily I watched the scenery alone.

Among oaks and chestnuts,
Hillside fruits were mostly tiny dots.
Some were red like cinnabar
Or black like lacquer spots.

From the rain and dew of Heaven,
Trees develop fruits, sweet or otherwise.
I thought of Peach Flower Stream.
Ill fate gave me more sighs.

Over the uneven lay of the land, I watched
    Fuzhou.
Peaks are followed by valleys downhill.
As I got near to the shore,
My servant was just by treetops uphill.

Owls hooted on yellow mulberry tree.
At scattered holes, field mice guarded, in
    the same mold.
I passed a battlefield well into the night
As moonlit white bones lay in the cold.

Our huge army at Tong Pass
Got quickly killed and torn apart.
Half of our countrymen were harmed and
    maimed,
Of the dead people of the other world, to
    be a part.

III

After being a captive of the rebels,
I returned to Fengxiang with white hair.

My wife and children were in rags
As I reached my thatched hut in a year.

Like sharp winds through pines, she wailed.
Like a cheerless brook, her quiet sobs had the
    same tempo.
My boy, the treasure of my life,
Had a complexion whiter than snow.

With no socks on his dirty feet,
He turned his back from me to weep.
Before the bed were my two little girls,
With patched robes and bare knees, for a
    lack of upkeep.

On an old piece of embroidery, patterns
    were not aligned.
Waves got ripped in the seascape.
Water Spirit and Purple Phoenix, on a
    short, coarse robe,
Got upside down in form and shape.

For days, I lay in bed with nausea and
    diarrhea,
In low spirits, being sick and old.
How can I not take out money from my
    trunk,
To save them from hunger and cold?

I took out rouge and powder from their
    packets,
Displaying my bedding, base and bare.
The face of my wife glowed again.
My mindless girls combed their hair.

They copied their mother's behavior.
Morning grooming was casually applied.
Their brows were painted too wide and
    uneven.
In a moment, rouge and powder were tried.

Returning alive before my young children,
I seem to forget about my hunger and
    thirst.
They asked me questions while pulling
    my beard.
Into a hollering rage, who could burst?

IV

His Majesty is still under exile.
How long with the rebels do we have to
    contend?
Looking up, I sense an auspicious sign
And feel the demonic energy will end.

Following the arduous Uighers,

A cold wind comes from the northwest.
Their king wants to help us,
With cavalries considered the best.

Five thousand soldiers will be sent
With ten thousand steeds.
It is preferable to use fewer Uighers
Who can conquer all with their brave
    and resolute steeds.

Fighters sent us act like soaring falcons
And can jump arrows in subduing their foe.
The sage ruler humbly waits for help.
Debates are thrown out of the window.

Luoyang can be easily recovered.
Changan, the West Capital, will succumb
    without a fight,
Our imperial army proposed an attack in
    penetration.
The joined forces will get in position with
    might.

We took Qingzhou and Xuzhou.
The recovery of Mount Heng and Jieshi Hill
    will follow.
It is time for dense, frosty dew in the sky.
The positive energy will deal rebels a deadly

blow.

Ill fate in turn befalls nomads this year.
In a month, they will be exterminated.
How long can they last?
The king's laws are not to be terminated.

V

Xuanzong handled a case different from the
    past.
I recall how the wretched history unfolded
    first.
He got a corrupt minister executed,
With his evil partners dispersed.

When Xia and Yin dynasties waned,
Their kings did not cause their famed
    consorts' demise.
Like Zhou and Han, our empire got
    revitalized.
Like Xuan and Guangwu, our emperor is
    really virtuous and wise.

Courageous general Chen Xuanli,
With loyalty, fought all the way.
Without him, all subjects would be dead.
The empire is still alive and well today.

Baishou Gate appears deserted.
Datong Palace is in a cheerless state.
People of the capital yearn for the king's
  return.
An aura of positive energy moves towards
  the Golden Gate.

For the spirits in royal mausoleums,
The practice of grave sweeping has always
  survived.
Brilliant is the work of Daizong.
His grand dynasty has thrived.

九成宮

蒼山入百里， 崖斷如杵臼。 曾宮憑風囘，
岌岸土囊口。 立神扶棟梁， 鑿翠開戶牖。
其陽產靈芝， 其陰宿牛斗。 紛披長松倒，
揭礜怪石走。 哀猿啼一聲， 客淚迸林藪。
荒哉隋家帝， 製此今頹朽。 向便國不亡，
焉為巨唐有。 雖無新增修， 尚置官居守。
巡非瑤水遠， 跡是雕牆後。 我行屬時危，
仰望嗟嘆久。 天王守太白， 駐馬更搔首。

Nine-Storied Palace

I saw a broken cliff like a pestle,
After going a hundred miles into the
   gray mountain.
This layered palace takes whirling winds,
High above a sac-like cave on the plain.

Deities are displayed near supporting rafters
   and beams.
Windows open to wall of foliage, lush and
   green.
On the sunlit south are grown lingzhis.
From the shady north, two stars, Niu and
   Dou, can be seen.

Odd-shaped rocks break free from tree
   stumps.
Upside down, tall pine branches spread.
At a single cry of a sad gibbon,
In groves and swamps, a wanderer's big
   tears are shed.

Indulged indeed was the Sui king
Who built this palace, now in decay.
Were it not for his fallen kingdom,
Our great Tang empire could not own it
   today.

Even without new additions or repairs,
There are still guards on site.
For royal visit, it is not as far as Yao Pool.
The record of indulgences is left with carved
walls in sight.

Looking up, I sigh and sigh with regret.
As I travel in these perilous times with wars
ahead.
Our heavenly king is hunting at Taibai.
I stay my horse and scratch my head.

收京三首，其一

仙仗離丹極，甘天照玉除。須為下殿走，
不可好樓居。暫屈汾陽駕，聊飛燕將書。
依然七廟略，更與萬方初。

Retaking the Capital, no.1

After the king and his guards left the palace,
On jade steps, the light of rebels, like demon
stars, has lain.
Forced to flee from his fine mansion,
He lived in a house, simple and plain.

The carriage took him to Fenyang.
A surrender appeal went to the rebel general
  of Yan.
The seven ancestral temples look intact.
A new beginning will be for all again.

收京三首，其二

生意甘衰白，天涯正寂寥。忽聞哀痛詔，
又下聖明朝。羽翼懷商老，文思憶帝堯。
叨逢罪己日，沾灑望青霄。

Retaking the Capital, no.2

I accept being frail and pale in my life,
Far from the capital and without any tie.
Suddenly from the sage, enlightened court,
I heard of an edict in sorrow and pain.
I recall recluses of Mount Shang who helped
  the young king
And King Yao's thoughts expressed in words
  in his reign.
With humility, I chance upon this day of
  self-blame.
In tears, I look at the blue sky.

收京三首，其三

汗馬收宮闕，春城鏟賊壕。賞應歌杕杜，
歸及薦櫻桃。雜虜橫戈數，功臣甲等高。
萬方頻送喜，無乃聖躬勞。

Retaking the Capital, no.3

We retook the palace with rare horses,
Ridding rebel trenches in the city in spring.
Returning troops were rewarded cherries.
"Russet Pear Tree" is a song they should sing.
The Uighers often use pikes in war.
Tall mansions are for meritorious ministers to
    gain.
Frequent good news comes from everywhere,
Due to the king's efforts in his sage reign.

Year 758

崔氏東山草堂

愛汝玉山草堂靜，高秋爽氣相鮮新。有時
自發鐘磬響，落日更見漁樵人。盤剝白鴉

谷口栗，飯煮青泥坊底芹。何為西莊王給事，柴門空閉鎖松筠。

Mister Cui's Thatched Cottage on East Hill

In cloudless fall, the air is crisp and fresh
I love your thatched cottage on East Hill so
    quiet.
At times, bells and musical stones sound.
Fishermen and woodcutters can be seen at
    sunset.
With rice is cooked celery from the Green
    Mud Neighborhood.
Peeled chestnuts from White Crow Valley
    are on a plate.
Why does Supervising Secretary Wang of
    West Villa
Pointlessly lock his pine and bamboo behind
    a humble gate?

廢畦

秋疏擁霜露，豈敢惜凋殘。暮景數枝葉，
天風吹汝寒。綠沾泥滓盡，香與歲時闌。
生意春如昨，悲君白玉盤。

Abandoned Plots

Fall vegetables get under dew and frost.
How dare I not lament the decay?
I count the leaves on shoots at twilight.
You are blown and chilled by Heaven's blast.
All the mud and mire are on the greens.
At this time of the year, your fragrance does
   not last.
Your liveliness belong to springtime of the
   past.
Under the bright full moon, with me sad
   thoughts stay.

木皮嶺

首路栗亭西，尚想鳳皇村。冬季攜童稚，
辛苦赴蜀門。南登木皮嶺，艱難不易論。
汗流被我體，祁寒為之暄。遠岫爭輔佐，
千巖自崩奔。始知五嶽外，別有他山尊。
仰干塞大明，俯入裂厚坤。再聞虎豹鬥，
屢蹈風水昏。高有廢閣道，摧折如短轅。
下有冬青林，石上走長根。西崖特秀發，
煥若靈芝繁。潤聚金碧氣，清無沙上痕。
憶觀昆侖圖，目擊玄圃存。對此欲何適，
默傷垂老魂。

Bark Ridge

I set out on the road west of Chestnut
  Pavilion.
In my heart, memories of Phoenix Village
  still stay.
I brought along young children in winter,
For our entry to Shu, with hardship on my
  way.

To the south, we climbed Bark Ridge.
The difficulties are hard to be told.
Sweat covered my body,
Warming me up in the severe cold.

Distant peaks fight to join one another.
Endless crags seem to break and run free.
Now I know beyond the Five Great
    Mountains,
There are other ones equally worthy.

They crack up the thick earth.
Big luminaries 阿 re blocked by the height.
Often uneasy with a dark windy shower,
I hear again tigers and leopards in fight.

Wrecked like a short carriage shaft,
High above, an abandoned plank road rests,
With long roots running on rocks.
Below I find evergreen forests.

The west slope is especially luxuriant,
Like clustered lingzhis, with a sheen.
There is a moist, dense aura of class,
    like gold and emerald.
Free from sand and dust, clear and clean.

I recall viewing a painting of Mount Kunlun,
With the mythical Fairyland still present.
Facing the ridge, where am I going?
With a wounded spirit, this aging man is
    silent.

東樓

萬里流沙道，西征過北門。但添新戰骨，
不返舊征魂。樓角淩風迴，城陰帶水昏。
傳聲看驛使，送節向河源。

East Tower

Those on western campaigns cross the North
   Gate.
For myriad miles, roads to the drifting sands
   go.
It only adds to the casualties in recent wars,
Without summoning the souls from battles
   long ago.
Wind whirls past the tower's corners.
On the dark waters, the city wall casts a
   shadow.
Pass the word around to catch sight of the
   envoy
Who goes towards the river's source with
   standards in tow.

空囊

翠柏苦猶食，　明霞朝可餐。　世人共鹵莽，
吾道屬艱難。　不爨井晨凍，　無衣床夜寒。
囊空恐羞澀，　留得一錢看。

The Empty Purse

Green, bitter cypress leaves can be a meal.
High, bright clouds can be my food.
Earthlings without principles get ahead.
My way of life makes difficult livelihood.
Dawn chill by the well sinks in when I do
　　not cook.
At night in bed, without blankets I feel cold.
An empty purse may be embarrassing.
Let me leave a copper coin for it to hold.

寄岳州賈司馬六丈巴州嚴八使君兩閣老五
十韻

衡岳啼猿裏，　巴州鳥道邊。　故人俱不利，
謫臣兩悠然。　開闢乾坤正，　榮枯雨露偏。
長沙才子遠，　釣籟客星懸。

II

憶昨趨行殿，
奉使待張騫。
蒼茫城七十，
旌頭俯澗廛。
浪作禽填海，
一鼓氣無前。
亂麻屍積衛，

殷憂捧禦筵。
無復雲臺仗，
流落劍三千。
小儒輕董卓，
那將血射天。
陰散陳倉北，
破竹勢臨燕。

討胡愁李廣，
虛修水戰船。
畫角吹秦晉，
有識笑符堅。
萬方思助順，
晴曛太白巔。

III

法駕還雙闕，
佳氣拂周旋。
侍臣諳入仗，
城凝碧樹煙。
哭廟悲風急，
春給水衡錢。
恩榮同拜手，
寒重繡被眠。

王師下八川。
貔虎開金甲，
廄馬解登仙。
衣冠心慘愴，
朝正霽景鮮。
內蕊繁於繢，
出入最隨肩。
彎齊兼秉燭，

此時沾奉引，
麒麟受玉鞭。
花動朱樓雪，
故老淚潺湲。
月分梁漢米，
宮莎軟勝綿。
晚著華堂醉，
書杠滿懷牋。

IV

每覺昇元輔，
鍛翮再聯翩。
青蒲甘受戮，

深期列大賢。
禁掖朋從改，
白髮竟誰憐？

秉鈞方咫尺，
微班性命全。
弟子貧原憲，

58

諸生老伏虔。師資謙未達，鄉黨敬何先？
舊好腸堪斷，新愁眼欲穿。翠乾危棧竹，
紅膩小湖蓮。賈筆論孤憤，嚴詩賦幾篇？
定知深意苦，莫使眾人傳。

V

貝錦無停織，朱絲有斷絃。浦鷗防碎首，
霜鶻不空拳。地僻昏炎瘴，山稠隘石泉。
且將棋度日，應用酒為年。典郡終微眇，
治中實棄捐。安排求傲吏，比興展歸田。
去去才難得，蒼蒼理又玄。古人稱逝矣，
吾道卜終焉。

VI

隴外翻投跡，漁陽復控弦。笑為妻子累，
甘與歲時遷。親故行稀少，兵戈動接連。
他鄉饒夢寐，失侶自迍邅。多病加淹泊，
長吟阻靜便。如公盡雄俊，志在必騰騫。

59

Sent to Two Senior Officials, Jia Zhi, the Sixth, Vice-Prefect of Yuezhou and Yan Wu, the Eighth, Prefect of Bazhou: Fifty Couplets

I

In Yuezhou, you can hear gibbons cry.
At Bazhou, trails are dangerous and narrow.
My old friends are both unlucky.
To faraway places in exile, you go.

The state began with forces of nature aligned.
With the king's kindness, you were down.
Jia Yi, a talented scholar, was exiled to
    Changsha afar.
The star of Yan Guang, the angler, worked
    against the crown.

II

I recall my last visit to the palace in exile
When I worked for the king in a nervous
    state.
We battle against foreign rebels without an
    able general like Li Guang.
For a loyal envoy like Zhang Qian, we have
    yet to wait.

Honor guards of Cloud Terrace are absent.
The old royal navy set up is now tossed.
Like the historical seventy cities, a huge area
    fell into enemy hands.
Three thousand soldiers were lost.

Mao Tou star, the omen for wars, is above
    Luoyang.
In Qin and Jin, painted war eagles are in
    play.
Minor scholars bypass usurper like Deng Zuo.
Learned people mock at the defeated
    chief, like Fu Jian of yesterday.

Like the bird trying to fill the sea, rebels
    misjudged,
Mistaking bloodshed for supremacy over
    Heaven gained.
Help from all over came for our just cause.
After the first attempt, the energy for combat
    never waned.

North of Chencang, black clouds dispersed.
At the peak of Mount Taibo, it was warm and
    sunlit.
Corpses of rebels piled up at Weizhou.
Our men headed towards Yan fast, like

bamboos split.

III

The royal army descended on the capital with
  eight rivers.
At the palace gates, the returning imperial
  coach was homebound.
At this time, to serve as an advisor to the king,
I felt good energy was swept all around.

Fierce and brave soldiers removed their metal
  armors.
Adorned with jade whips, unicorn-like steeds
  stand.
Attendant officials were familiar with setting
  up honor guards.
By horses from the Royal Stables, the way to
  Fairyland was understood.

Flowers shake off snow on crimson towers.
Mist on green trees covered the whole city.
Officials in formal wear were grieved at
  Heart.
Tears of elders ran free.

Making sacrifices at the ancestral temple,
  the king wept in a blast.

To the court, a fresh start was what the
    sunlit scene could bring.
Each month, ministers were allotted Liang
    Han rice.
And cash minted by the Shu Heng office in
    spring.

Flowers in the inner court number more than
    silk ribbon knots.
Softer than cotton, sedge grows in the palace.
Basked in grace, we three bowed to His
    Majesty.
Entering or leaving, we walked together,
    shoulder to shoulder, at the same pace.

Under embroidered quilts, we sleep in the
    severe cold,
Having got drunk late in the day.
We rode bridle to bridle, holding candles.
I have an armful of letters you sent me out
    of your way.

IV

I always think of your promotion to the very
    top
And deeply hope, among the great sages,
    you will stay.

Despite wrecked feathers, you will flit
   together again.
Holding the ultimate rein of government is
   but a foot away.

Friends and associates in the palace bureaus
   change.
In a minor post, I got my life spared.
I braved death and spoke up to the king.
Who pities this man who is white-haired?

Yuan Xian was the poorest disciple
While Fu Qian was the oldest.
I humbly deny being a qualified teacher.
Why do fellow villagers respect me more
   than the rest?

The plight of my old friends is heart-breaking.
New sources of sorrow make me teary.
Green bamboos for the perilous plank roads
   became dry.
Red lotus blooms of a small lake look weary.

Jia Yi wrote about solitude and anger.
How many new poems has Yan Wu done?
I know well how bitter you feel.
Do not share it with everyone.

V

Like weaving rare brocade, rumors from
   slanderers never stop.
Crimson threads of justice can break.
Gulls by the shore guard against crushed
   skulls.
In failed attacks, birds of prey in the frost
   never partake.

Ruling a county is in the end insignificant.
A prefect's job can easily be cast aside.
A proud official resigned to live in his own
   way.
By your interest to your fields at home,
   you should abide.

Springs among rocks can hardly flow in
   this hilly place.
The remote spot is hot and dark, with miasma
   everywhere.
Spend your days on chess
And drink wine from year to year.

With rare talent, you are leaving us.
The logic of life is not openly and clearly
   designed.
An ancient left his office, feeling in disfavor.

My destiny is to be divined.

VI

My tracks are beyond local fields in the
    country.
Yuyang, the rebel base, is war-ready.
I may be jeered for being held back by my
    family,
But I accept change that is time-based and
    steady.

On my trip, friends and relatives are fewer.
Protracted wars get out of hand.
Without a friend, I find the journey difficult.
I sleep and dream a lot in a strange land.

Chanting for long blocks moments of
    quietude and ease.
Frequent illnesses detain me more.
Gentlemen like you are all outstanding
    heroes.
You will surely aim high as you soar.

發潭州

夜醉長沙酒，曉行湘水春。岸花飛送客，
檣燕語留人。賈傅才未有，褚公書絕倫。
高名前後事，回首一傷神。

Setting out from Tanzhou

I get drunk at night on Changsha wine,
Sailing at dawn on River Xiang on a spring
   day.
Flying petals from the shore see me off.
Swallows by the mast ask me to stay.
Exiled to Tanzhou were Jia Yi, a talented
   tutor,
And Chu Suiliang, a top calligrapher of
   yesterday.
With great fame, they suffered at different
   times.
On looking back, I feel depressed in the
   same way.

赤谷

天寒霜雪繁，遊子有所之。豈但歲月暮，
重來未有期。晨發赤谷亭，險艱方自茲。

亂石無改轍，我車已載脂。山深苦多風，
落日童稚飢。悄然村墟迴，煙火何由追。
貧病轉零落，故鄉不可思。常恐死道路，
永為高人嗤。

Red Valley

Frost and snow are heavy in the cold.
I am the traveler going somewhere.
Not only is it getting late in the year,
But to return here, I did not prepare.

At dawn, I set out for Red Valley Station.
From there, the journey will be hard.
A detour is impossible among jumbled rocks.
On my cart, I have carried lard.

To our woe, deep in the hill it is very windy.
My children are hungry at sunset.
How can we trace the source of hearth fire
When silence and distance shut me off from
    any hamlet?

Poor and sick, I feel more lost,
Unable to think of my hometown.
I always fear of death on the road
And forever, by lofty people, being put down.

立秋後題

日月不相饒，節序昨夜隔。玄蟬無停號，
秋燕已如客。平生獨往願，悵年半百。
罷官亦由人，何事拘形役。

Written after the Beginning of Autumn

Time does not cut some slack.
Last night, a seasonal change was addressed.
Black cicadas do not stop their cries.
Each fall swallow is already a departed guest.
For my whole life, I wish to set out alone.
That my age is fifty leaves me depressed.
I can decide on resigning from office.
To labor myself, why am I so hard pressed?

Year 760-764

將曉二首，其一

石城除擊柝，鐵鎖欲開關。鼓角悲荒塞，
星河落曙山。巴人常小梗，蜀使動無還。
垂老孤帆色，飄飄犯百蠻。

Approaching Dawn in Two Poems, no.1

The sound of watch clappers stops on stone
 walls.
Without iron locks, they are about to open
 the gate.

The Milky Way is gone beyond dawn hills.
The deserted frontier, with bugle and drum,
 is in a cheerless state.
Envoys sent to Shu never return,
To settle small social problems Ba folks
 create.
I am an aging trespasser with a lone sail,
 drifting along.
To the natives of many tribes here, I cannot
 relate.

將曉二首，其二

軍吏囘官燭，舟人自楚歌。塞沙蒙薄霧，
落月去清波。壯惜身名晚，衰慚應接多。
歸朝日簪笏，筋力定如何。

Approaching Dawn in Two Poems, no.2

Boatmen break into songs of Chu.

With official torches, a returning orderly is
  on his way.
Cold sands get a veil of thin mist.
Among clear waves, the sinking moon cannot
  stay.
Frequent social events make my weak body
  feel embarrassed.
Regrettably, at my prime, fame is still in
  delay.
Can my strength really handle it?
Returning to court, I shall hold a tablet,
With my pen on my headdress each day.

蕭八明府實處覓桃栽

奉乞桃栽一百根，春前為送浣花村。河陽
縣裏雖無數，濯錦江邊未滿園。

Asking for Peach Saplings from County Magistrate Xiao Shi, the Eighth

For a hundred peach saplings, I beg of you,
To be sent to Flower Washing Village, before
  spring is through.
My garden by Brocade Rinsing River still
  has room.

In Heyang County in the past, countless peach trees grew.

從韋二明府續處覓棉竹

華軒藹藹他年到，綿竹亭亭出縣高。江上舍前無此物，幸分蒼翠拂波濤。

Asking for "Silken Bamboos" from County Magistrate Wei Xu, the Second

My visit to your grand porch will be in a future year.
In the county, slim silken bamboos stand tall and fair.
My riverside cottage has nothing like them.
Bright green leaves would brush waves if by luck I could get a share.

憑韋少府班覓松樹子栽

落落出群非欅柳，青青不朽豈楊梅。欲存老蓋千年意，為覓霜根數寸栽。

Asking Sheriff Wei Ban for a Pine Seedling for Planting

The elm does not spread wide or stand out.
The arbutus is not an evergreen tree.
I want to keep a mature canopy that suggests
　　antiquity.
Several inches of frosty roots for planting are
　　sought by me.

嚴公廳宴同詠蜀道畫圖　（得空字）

日臨公館靜。畫滿地圖雄。劍閣星橋北，
松州雪嶺東。華夷山不斷，吳蜀水相連。
興與煙霞會，清樽幸不空。

At a Feast in the Mansion of Lord Yan, we All Compose poems on a Painting of Shu Trails (My Allotted Word is "Empty")

The painting of Shu trails is detailed and
　　grand.
The mansion is sunlit, without a sound.
Sword Pavilion is north of Star Bridge.
East of snowy ridges, Songzhou is found.
Rivers in Wu and Shu join.
Hills do not break from Chinese to nomad

ground.
It is our pleasure to meet amid mist and cloud
And luck with no empty wine goblets around.

江亭王閬州筵餞蕭遂州

離亭非舊國，春色是他鄉。老畏歌聲斷，
愁隨舞曲長。二天開寵餞，五馬爛生光。
川路風煙接，俱宜下鳳凰。

At a River Pavilion, Wang of Langzhou Holds a Parting Feast for Xiao of Suizhou

The beauty of spring belongs to another land.
It is no hometown at the pavilion of parting
    here.
My grief follows the length of long dancing
    tunes.
The end of singing gives this old man fear.
The guest dazzles us with his five-horse
    entourage.
It is a "Two Horses" feast for a friend held
    dear.
The road to Sichuan is windy and misty.
As rare phoenixes, both of you are apt to
    appear.

東津送韋諷攝閬州錄事

聞說江山好，憐君吏隱兼。寵行舟遠泛，
怯別酒頻添。推薦非承乏，超持必去嫌。
他時如按縣，不得慢陶潛。

At East Ford, Seeing off Wei Feng Who is Taking up the Post of Office Manager in Langzhou

From hearsay I know of the fine scenery there
Where I love you can combine your job and
    retirement.
Your send-off on a far voyage is much
    pampered.
Afraid of parting, we keep more refills of ale.
Your recommended job is not one to fill a
    void.
In holding your post, you must rid any
    resentment.
Should anyone inspect your county some day,
To respect your life style after Tao Qian, he
    must not fail.

陪諸公上白帝城頭宴越公堂之作

此堂存古製，城上俯江郊。落構垂雲雨，
荒階蔓草茅。柱穿蜂溜蜜，棧缺燕添巢。
坐接春杯氣，心傷艷蕊梢。英靈如過隙，
宴衍願投膠。莫問東流水，生涯未即拋。

Accompanied by Various Gentlemen, I Climb atop the Wall of White Emperor Fortress and Share a Feast in the Hall of Duke of Yue

This hall, in its original construction,
Commands a view of the riverside outskirts
　below.
The fallen frame hangs on amid cloud and
　rain.
On deserted steps, rank grasses grow.
Through pierced pillars comes honey oozed
　from bees.
Each gap of plank walkways is added the
　nest of the swallow.
In spring I sit to share the spirit through
　passing the wine cup.
For blooms at branch tips, I am in pain and
　sorrow.
After this happy feast, I wish to be bonded
　like glue

With heroic souls quickly on the go.
I am not ready to quit this mortal life.
Ask not of the river in its unending eastward
    flow.

大麥行

大麥乾枯小麥黃，婦女行泣夫走藏。東至
集壁西梁洋，問誰腰鎌胡與羌。豈無蜀兵
三千人，簿領辛苦江山長。安得如鳥有翅
膀，託身白雲還故鄉。

Ballad of Barley

With yellow wheat and dry barley in decay,
Women walk in tears as men run for a
    hideaway.
From Jizhou to Bizhou in the east to
    Liangzhou and Yangzhou in the west,
If you ask, nomads with sickles at their waists
    make a foray.
Three thousand Shu soldiers, as relief forces
    in hardship,
Have been led past river and hill far away.
How can we have wings like birds
And return to our hometowns on white

clouds all the way?

光祿阪行

山行落日下絕壁，西望千山萬山赤。樹枝
有鳥亂鳴時，暝色無人獨歸客。馬驚不憂
深谷墜，草動只怕長弓射。安得更似開元
中，道路即今多擁隔。

Ballad of the Guanglu's Slope

I walk in the hills with sunset past a sheer
  cliff.
As I look west, countless hills emit a red
  glow.
Birds in tree branches call in confusion.
A stranger returns in the dark alone.
On a startled horse, I worry not about falling
  into a deep valley.
As grass moves, I feel only being shot by a
  long bow.
Right how, most roads are blocked.
How can we model again the Kaiyuan reign
  years ago?

為農

錦里煙塵外，江村八九家。圓荷浮小葉，
細麥落輕花。卜宅從茲老，為農去國賒。
遠慚勾漏令，不得問丹砂。

Being a Farmer

Past the smoke and dust of Chengdu,
There are riverside villages with eight to nine
    families or so.
Round lotuses let their small leaves float.
Light flowers of tiny wheat fall to the
    soil below.
This is the hut for me to age as a farmer.
Unfulfilled, away from the capital I go.
I have not found an elixir for immortality,
To be shamed by Goulan's magistrate, an
    alchemist of ages ago.

上白帝城

城峻隨天壁，樓高更女牆。江流思夏后，
風至憶襄王。老去聞悲角，人扶報夕陽。
公孫初恃險，躍馬意何長。

Climbing White Emperor Fortress

Steep walls follow the contour of sky-high
cliffs.
By battlements, the lofty towers are set.
I think of King Yu of Xia by the river's flow,
And King Xiang as winds blow, with a
nostalgic mindset.
To my old ears, bugles sound cheerless.
Propped by others, I hear of another sunset.
Here Gongsun Shu once relied on this
military vantage point.
For the crown, how ambitious was his bet!

上白帝城二首，其一

江城含變態，一上一回新。天欲今朝雨，
山歸萬古春。英雄餘事業，衰邁夕風塵。
取醉他鄉客，相逢故國人。兵戈猶擁蜀，
賦斂強輸秦。不是煩形勝，深愧畏損神

Climbing White Emperor Fortress in Two Poems, no.1

The riverside fortress offers changing, novel
views.
As you climb and circle at each height.

The sky is about to rain at dawn.
Hills are forever spring-like to my sight.
Heroes have left their marks in history.
Long amid wind and dust, I waste away.
Meeting people from my hometown,
Let me get drunk in this adopted land I stay.
Warfare still goes on in Shu.
Taxes are levied by the brutes in our name.
I am not tired of scenic spots,
But the fear of sapping my energy gives me
    great shame.

上白帝城兩首，其二

白帝空祠廟，孤雲自往來。江山城苑轉，
棟宇客徘徊。勇略今何在，當年亦壯哉。
後人將酒肉，虛殿日塵埃。谷鳥鳴還過，
林花落又開。多慚病無力，騎馬入青苔。

Climbing White Emperor Fortress in Two Poems, no.2

Above the empty shrine of White Emperor
    Fortress,
Isolated clouds come and go.
The riverside fortress is on a winding road

uphill.
Before buildings, tourists pace to and fro.
Where are those brave schemers now?
How ambitious they were years ago!
Men offer meat and wine as libation today.
The deserted hall gets more dust each day.
Birdsongs from the valley start and stop.
In cycles, blooms in groves open and drop.
Onto green moss, I proceed on horseback,
Much ashamed of the health and strength I
  lack.

溪漲

當時浣水橋，溪水繞尺餘。白石明可把，
水中有行車。秋夏忽泛溢，豈惟入吾廬。
絞龍亦狼狽，況是鱉與魚。茲晨已半落，
歸路跬步疏。馬嘶未敢動，前有深填淤。
青青屋東麻，散亂床上書。不知遠山雨，
夜來復何如。我遊都市間，晚憩比村墟。
乃知久行客，終日思其居。

The Creek Floods

Back then at the bridge of my village,

The creek was just over a foot in height.
People could move wagons in the waters.
And handpick pebbles that looked bright.
It suddenly flooded over in late summer,
Not just into my cottage on one site.
Even flood dragons felt wretched,
Let alone turtles and fish in the same
     plight.
This morn, it has half-subsided.
On the returning path, few travelers are in
     sight.
Deep mud lies in front.
Horses dare not move but just neigh.
East of the cottage is green hemp.
On my bed are books in disarray.
I do not know if the rain in the far hills
Will be here again at night.
When I go visiting in the city,
Be evening, in a village I always stay for my
     respite.
Now I realize for a long-term wanderer,
All day, the thought of lodging is wound tight.

新秋

火雲猶未斂奇峰，欹枕初驚一葉風。幾處
園林蕭瑟裏，誰家砧杵寂寥中。蟬聲斷續
悲殘月，螢燄高低照暮空。賦就金門期再
獻，夜深搔首歎飛蓬。

Early Autumn

Fiery clouds at awesome peaks are still in
　　sight.
Reclining on a pillow, from a slight wind I
　　first take fright.
From which family comes the sound of the
　　mallet in the quietude.
Groves look desolate at each site.
On and off, cicadas chirp under a cheerless,
　　waning moon.
High and low, fireflies move with their glow
　　at twilight.
I hope to present a poem again through the
　　Golden Light Gate.
I scratch my head and sigh, looking like a
　　tumbleweed, late at night.

秋盡

秋盡東行且未廻，茅齋寄在少城隈。籬邊
老卻陶潛菊，江上徒逢袁紹杯。雪嶺獨看
西日落，劍門猶阻北人來。不辭萬里長為
客，懷抱何時得好開。

End of Autumn

My thatched cottage is in a corner of "Small
City".
At fall's end, in my eastern trip, I have not
returned yet.
My chrysanthemums resemble those of Tao
Qian by the hedge.
On the river, a benefactor, like Yuan Shao,
is hard to get.
Swordgate Pass still blocks people from the
north.
At a snowy ridge, I watch west alone for
sunset.
For myriad miles, I have not refused being a
long-term wanderer.
When will my heart stop being upset?

十二月一日三首，其一

今朝臘月春意動，雲安縣前江可憐。一聲
何處送書雁，百丈誰家上水船。未將梅蕊
驚愁眼，要取椒花媚遠天。明光起草人所
羨，肺病幾時朝日邊。

The First Day of the Twelfth Month in Three Poems, no.1

Fronting Yunan County, the dawn river looks
   lovely,
In winter's last month, with active signs of
   spring.
Where comes the single cry of the wild goose
   with letters?
Whose is it, a distance away, a boat upstream
   going?
Soon I shall use pepper flowers to flirt with
   the faraway sky,
Not yet in sadness to see amazing plums
   flowering.
Drafters of edicts in Mingguang Palace are
   envied by others.
With sick lungs, when will I get to be near
   the king?

十二月一日三首，其二

寒輕市上山煙碧，日滿樓前江霧黃。負鹽
出井此溪女，打鼓發船何郡郎。新亭舉目
風景切，茂陵著書消渴長。春花不愁不爛
漫，楚客唯聽樣相將。

The First Day of the Twelfth Month in Three Poems, no.2

With a light chill over the market, the hill
looks misty and green.
Before a riverside tower, the fully sunlit fog
appears yellow.
Girls of the creek carry salt from the wells.
Lads of an unknown county set sail as drum
beats go.
Like Jin people at New Pavilion, I gaze hard
at my lost homeland.
Like Sima Xiangru of Maoling, I write so the
king would know.
I care less about spring blooms not showy.
The sound of oars is only what the ears of
a wanderer follow.

十二月一日三首，其三

即看燕子入山扉，豈有黃鸝歷翠微。短短
桃花臨水岸，輕輕柳絮點人衣。春來准擬
開懷久，老去親知見面稀。他日一杯難強
進，重嗟筋力故山遠。

The First Day of the Twelfth Month in Three Poems, no.3

Soon swallows coming between peaks will be
   in sight.
How can we miss orioles passing verdant
   foliage from site to site?
Hanging over the bank by waters are short
   Peach flowering twigs.
Touching our robes are willow fluff so light.
Old, I know well about rare reunions.
With spring coming, I plan hard to prolong
   my delight.
A cup of wine will be hard to be forced down
   in future.
I sigh again that my strength and distant
   hometown do not match right.

江頭五詠，丁香

丁香體柔羽，亂結枝猶墊。細葉帶浮毛，
疏花披素艷。深栽小齋後，庶近幽人占。
晚墮蘭麝中，休懷粉身念

Five Songs by the River: Cloves

The clove has a soft, weak structure,
With twigs still overwhelmed while tangled
    in a mess.
Its small leaves are covered by down.
Each rare bloom wears a pretty white dress.
Planted deep behind my small study,
It is almost something a hermit wants to
    possess.
As for finally falling for orchid and musk,
Any concern for this powdered plant body,
    I cease to address.

江頭五詠：梔子

梔子比眾木，人間誠未多。於身色有用，
與道氣傷和。紅取風霜實，青看雨露柯。
無情移得汝，貴在映江波。

Five Songs by the River: Gardenias

Compared with other plants, gardenias,
In the human world, are really few.
In healthy living, it harms the harmony of
 bodily functions.
From its structure, the usefulness is its hue.
I praise the red seeds after wind and frost
And green twigs in rain and dew.
With boundless zeal, I transplanted you.
Against river waves, rare is your reflection
 in view,

江頭五詠：花鴨

花鴨無泥滓，階前每緩行。羽毛知獨立，
黑白太分明。不覺群心妒，休牽眾眼驚。
稻粱沾汝在，作意莫先鳴。

Five Songs by the River: Mottled Duck

The mottled duck is without mud or dirt,
Always walking slowly by my stair.
The black and white shades are too distinct.
Of its unique feathers, it is aware.
It is not cognizant of the jealousy of the
 crowd.

I advise against your causing any stare.
You are favored by the grains here.
Not to be the first to sound off, you should
    take care.

江頭五詠：麗春

百草競春華，麗春應最勝。少須好顏色，
多漫枝條剩。紛紛桃李枝，處處總能移。
如何貴比重，卻怕有人知。

Five Songs by the River：Li Chun

All plants compete in spring flowering.
Championship is what Li Chun should
    obtain.
Those few in numbers need good colors.
Excessive twigs are mostly in vain.
Peach and pear, with branches in profusion,
Can be transplanted everywhere in the main.
How do you make judgments of worth?
The fear that someone knows about it is the
    issue that may pertain.

江頭五詠：鸂鶒

故使籠寬織。須指動損毛。看雲莫悵望，
失水任呼號。六翮曾經剪，孤飛卒未高。
且無鷹隼慮，留滯莫辭勞。

Five Songs by the River: Xi Chi

On purpose, I weave a wide cage.
That moving can harm your feathers, I know.
Do not get depressed looking at clouds.
Out of water, sound out in the manner you
  want to follow.
Your wings have been clipped.
Your lone flight is still low.
There is no worry about hawks and kites.
Your chance for a long stay here is not what
  you should forego.

五盤

五盤雖云險，山色佳有餘。仰淩棧道細，
俯映江木疏。地僻無網罟，水清反多魚。
好鳥不妄飛，野人半巢居。喜見淳樸俗，
坦然心神舒。東郊尚格鬥，巨猾何時除。

故鄉有弟妹，流落隨丘墟。成都萬事好，
豈若歸吾廬。

Five Switchbacks

The colorful hills look unusually fine
Though "Five Switchbacks" is dangerous,
 from hearsay.
Sparse trees below by the river emit a glow.
Across the slope above runs a narrow
 plank road.
More fish crowd the limpid waters.
This land has no nets or snares, being
 out-of-the-way.
Smart birds do not fly headlong.
In haunts, half of the rustics stay.
I feel relaxed and soothed in mind and spirit,
Glad to see pure and simple customs in play.
War still goes on in the eastern suburbs.
When can we drive big, slick rebels away?
My hometown where I had brothers and
 sisters
Is now in ruins, with us as wanderers away.
How can Chengdu compare to going home
Even if this city looks good in every way?

贈鄭十八賁

溫溫士君子，　令我懷抱盡。　靈芝冠眾芳，
安得闕親近。　遭亂意不歸，　竄身跡非隱。
細人尚姑息，　吾子色愈謹。　高懷見物理，
識者安肯哂。　卑飛欲何待，　捷徑應未忍。
示我百篇文，　詩家一標準，　羈離交屈宋，
牢落值顏閔。　水陸迷畏途，　藥餌駐修軫。
古人日以遠，　青史字不泯。　步趾詠唐虞，
追隨飯葵菫。　數杯資好事，　異味煩縣伊。
心雖在朝謁，　力與願矛盾。　抱病排金門，
衰容豈為敏。

For Zheng Bi, the Eighteenth

The mild manners of this fine gentleman
Holds the ultimate admiration from my mind.
You are a lingzhi that tops all fragrant herbs.
To be near you, how can I fall behind?

In turmoil, you do not want to return.
You are no hermit, though mostly out of sight.
Petty people seek indulgence over leniency.
You look more cautious to be proper and
　　upright.

Your loftiness lends you the vision for

principles.
How can those in the know hold you in
    disdain?
What are you waiting for, in your humble
    post?
Shortcuts are not what you care to gain.

You showed me a hundred pieces of writings.
That is the standard for poets you set.
As a detained wanderer, I form ties with Qu
    Yuan and Song Yu.
Down and out, to meet Yan Hui and Minzi
    Qian, I want to get.

I stop my cart for medicine.
On dangerous land and water routes, I get
    astray.
Words in history will not perish.
Ancients are leaving us still further each day.

I chant in praise of King Yu as I go about.
To pursue my ideals, I dine on mallows.
A few cups help create good experiences.
I trouble the county chief for a different trade
    my skill follows.

My strength and my wishes are conflicting,
Though the hope to go to the court is firm

in my heart.
In sickness to wait at the Golden Light Gate,
For me with an aging face, is hardly smart.

四松

四松初移時，　大抵三尺強。　別來忽三載，
離立如人長。　會看根不拔，　莫計枝凋傷。
幽色華秀發，　疏柯亦昂藏。　所插小藩籬，
本亦有堤防。　終然振撥損，　得愧千葉黃。
敢為故林主，　黎庶猶未康。　避賊今始歸，
春草滿空堂。　覽物歎衰謝，　及茲慰淒涼。
清風為我起，　灑面若微霜。　足以送老姿，
聊待偃蓋張。　我生無根蒂，　配爾亦茫茫。
有情且賦詩，　事跡可兩忘。　勿矜千載後，
慘澹蟠穹蒼。

Four Pines

The four pines when first transplanted
Were a little over three feet tall.
It has been three years since I left them.
They now assume a man's height overall.

So long as they are not uprooted,

I worry not about their shoots in decay.
Quietly their color and shape look charming.
Sparse branches grow in a dignified way.

The little hedge that I planted
Gave protection at the start.
In the end, it got swiped and hurt,
With countless yellow leaves, to my shameful
    heart.

I dare not claim ownership of this old grove
When from wars, commoners have not
    recovered.
I have just come as a refugee from rebels.
With spring grass, my empty hall is fully
    covered.

Accessing these tree consoles me in grief.
I sigh as all in my view can fade away.
A cool wind rises for me,
Like spring frost on my face in a spray.

They are enough to accompany me as I age.
I wait for spreading canopies as twigs mature.
In this life, I am rootless.
To share the same space and time with them
    is unsure.

Let me write a poem on my feelings.
What happened can be mutually forgotten.
Do not boast how a thousand years from now,
In the gray sky, sad and bleak, how coiled up
   you will have gotten.

自閬州領妻子卻赴蜀山行三首，其一

汩汩避群盜，悠悠經十年。不成向南國，
復作遊西川。物役水虛照，魂傷山寂然。
我生無倚著，盡室畏途邊。

From Langzhou I Take my Wife and Children back to Shu, Traveling in the Mountain, no.1

In confusion, we fled the rebels.
Slowly it has been ten years in a chain.
I did not manage going to the southern lands.
We were journeying to West River again.
The material world enslaves me; waters
   soothe me in vain.
My spirit is wounded in the quiet mountain.
The whole family moves on perilous paths.
In my whole life, there is no support to gain.

自閬州領妻子卻赴蜀山行三首，其二

長林偃風色，迴復意又迷。衫裏翠微潤，
馬銜青草嘶。棧懸斜避石，橋斷卻尋溪。
何日干戈盡，飄飄愧對妻。

From Langzhou I Take my Wife and Children back to Shu, Traveling in the Mountain, no.2

The tall forest blocks winds and colors.
Making my rounds, I feel carried away.
My robe gets wet amid the moist verdure.
With green grass in their mouths, horses
    neigh.
The broken bridge prompts me to seek a
    crossing over the creek.
To dodge rocks, they hang aslant each
    plank on the way.
Uprooted, I feel shame before my wife.
For peace, when is the day?

自閬州領妻子卻赴蜀山行三首，其三

行色遞隱見，人煙時有無。僕夫穿竹語，
稚子入雲呼。轉石驚魑魅，抨弓落狖鼯。
真拱一笑樂，似欲慰窮途。

From Langzhou I Take my Wife and Children back to Shu, Traveling in the Mountain, no.3

I see other travelers on and off.
Cooking smoke from homes comes in and out
  of sight.
My servant talks through bamboos.
My boy shouts to the clouds at a height.
Twanged bows bring down gibbons and
  flying squirrels.
Tumbling rocks give goblins fright.
As if to pacify our hardship of travel,
These really provide us with a moment of
  laughter in delight.

承聞河北諸道節度入朝歡喜口號絕句十二
首，其一

祿山作逆降天誅，更有思明亦已無。洶洶
人寰猶不定，時時鬥戰欲何須。

**Hearing that the Military Commissioner of
All the Circuits of Hebei Have Come to
Court, I am Delighted and Write Twelve
Extempore Quatrains, no.1**

An Lushan, the rebel, got Heaven's
    punishments acted upon.
Also Shi Siming is already gone.
The unrest among our people is not settled.
What is the need of battles going on and on?

承聞河北諸道節度入朝歡喜口號絕句十二
首，其二

社稷蒼生計必安，蠻夷雜種錯相干。周宣
漢武今王是，孝子忠臣後代看。

101

Hearing that the Military Commissioner of All the Circuits of Hebei Have Come to Court, I am Delighted and Write Twelve Extempore Quatrains, no.2

For peace, the national plan must be.
With us, nomad bastards err by being at
    enmity.
The present king matches King Xuan of Zhou
    and King Wu of Han.
Posterity will judge us by our filial piety and
    loyalty.

承聞河北諸道節度入朝歡喜口號絕句十二
首，其三

喧喧道路多歌謠，河北將軍盡入朝。始是
乾坤王室正，卻交江漢客魂銷。

Hearing that the Military Commissioner of All the Circuits of Hebei Have Come to Court, I am Delighted and Write Twelve Extempore Quatrains, no.3

Noisily much singing erupts on the pathway.
Every general from Hebei comes to the court
    all the way.

It started with the restored legitimacy of the
monarchy,
But got the mood of a wanderer of Yangzi
and Han carried away.

承聞河北諸道節度入朝歡喜口號絕句十二
首，其四

不論諸公無表來，茫然庶事遣人猜。擁兵
相學干戈銳，使者徒勞百萬廻。

**Hearing that the Military Commissioner of
All the Circuits of Hebei Have Come to
Court, I am Delighted and Write Twelve
Extempore Quatrains, no.4**

It matters not without petitions these
gentlemen have come.
Quizzical about their sundry matters, we have
become.
With their own armies, they copy one another
in sharp weaponry.
For countless times, court emissaries failed in
the outcome.

承聞河北諸道節度入朝歡喜口號絕句十二
首，其五

嗚玉鏘金盡正臣，修文偃武不無人。興王
會靜妖氛氣，聖壽宜過十萬春。

**Hearing that the Military Commissioner of
All the Circuits of Hebei Have Come to
Court, I am Delighted and Write Twelve
Extempore Quatrains, no.5**

Jade and gold chimes clang; all your officials
    look upright.
You promote culture over wars; able men are
    in sight.
May our king of the restoration clean out the
    aura of witchery.
That His Majesty will live beyond ten
    thousand springs sounds right.

承聞河北諸道節度入朝歡喜口號絕句十二
首，其六

英雄見事若通神，聖哲為心小一身。燕趙
休矜出佳麗，宮闈不擬選才人。

Hearing that the Military Commissioner of All the Circuits of Hebei Have Come to Court, I am Delighted and Write Twelve Extempore Quatrains, no.6

As if communicating with the gods, a hero
    sets his insight.
In minding affairs, the self-image of a sage
    ruler is slight.
May Yan and Zhou warlords stop bragging
    and exporting beauties.
The timing to pick them as ladies-in-waiting
    in our palace is not right.

承聞河北諸道節度入朝歡喜口號絕句十二
首，其七

抱病江天白首郎，空山樓閣暮春光。衣冠
是日朝天子，草奏何時入帝鄉。

Hearing that the Military Commissioner of All the Circuits of Hebei Have Come to Court, I am Delighted and Write Twelve Extempore Quatrains, no.7

Sick by the river, I have a head of white hair.
At twilight in spring, by a tower the hill looks

bare.

On this day, in caps and gowns, they pay
respects to the crown.

When will I enter the palace for my drafted
petition to share?

承聞河北諸道節度入朝歡喜口號絕句十二
首，其八

澶漫山東一百州，削成如桉抱青丘。苞茅
重入歸關內，王祭還供盡海頭。

Hearing that the Military Commissioner of All the Circuits of Hebei Have Come to Court, I am Delighted and Write Twelve Extempore Quatrains, no.8

East of the mountain, a hundred prefectures
spread out calmly.

Pared flat like a table, in the embrace of green
hills.

Within the passes, special herbs as tributes
reappear,

For palace sacrifices, all the way to the edge
of the sea.

承聞河北諸道節度入朝歡喜口號絕句十二
首，其九

東逾遼水北滹沱，星象風雲喜共和。紫氣
關臨天地濶，黃金臺貯俊賢多。

**Hearing that the Military Commissioner of
All the Circuits of Hebei Have Come to
Court, I am Delighted and Write Twelve
Extempore Quatrains, no.9**

Past Liao's waters in the east and River
  Hutuo in the north,
Star omens and politics happily bring peace
  in place.
From the passes, an aura of royalty in purple
  hangs over our wide universe.
Many men of rare talent are recruited at the
  Golden Terrace.

承聞河北諸道節度入朝歡喜口號絕句十二
首，其十

漁陽突騎邯鄲兒，酒酣並轡金鞭垂。意氣
即歸雙闕舞，雄豪復遣五陵和。

Hearing that the Military Commissioner of All the Circuits of Hebei Have Come to Court, I am Delighted and Write Twelve Extempore Quatrains, no.10

The sallying cavalries of Yuyang and the
  lads of Handan,
With their idle golden whips, ride side by
  side, looking tipsy.
In high spirits, on return they instantly dance
  with obeisance in the palace.
Our tough youngsters of Wuling need to
  match their war-like audacity.

承聞河北諸道節度入朝歡喜口號絕句十二
首，其十一

李相將軍擁薊門，白頭雖老赤心存。竟能
盡說諸侯入，知有從來天子尊。

Hearing that the Military Commissioner of All the Circuits of Hebei Have Come to Court, I am Delighted and Write Twelve Extempore Quatrains, no.11

General Li Guangbi held Jimen.
Though old and white haired, he retained

his loyalty.
He could persuade all the lords to come to
the palace
And make them realize the Son of Heaven's
enduring supremacy.

承聞河北諸道節度入朝歡喜口號絕句十二
首，其十二

十二年來多戰場，天威已息陣堂堂。神靈
漢代中興主，功業汾陽異姓王。

Hearing that the Military Commissioner of All the Circuits of Hebei Have Come to Court, I am Delighted and Write Twelve Extempore Quatrains, no.12

For twelve years, many conflicts on
battlefields came.
With grand army formations, the monarch's
sternness has become tame.
The divine king of restoration matches those
of Han times.
A meritorious general was made the Prince
of Fenyang with a different surname.

熱，其一

雷霆空霹靂，雲雨竟虛無。赤赫衣流汗，
低垂氣不蘇。乞為寒水玉，願作冷秋菰。
何以兒童戲，風涼出舞雩。

Heat, no.1

There are peals of empty loud thunders,
Without cloud and rain still.
Sweat streams down people's robes.
They hang their heads low, with energy spent.
I beg to be jade in cold water
And hope to be a mushroom in the fall chill.
How can this compare to my childhood years
When out of the Rain Altar, in a cold wind
　　I went.

熱，其二

瘴雲終不減，瀘水復西來。閉戶人高臥，
歸林鳥卻回。峽中都似火，江上只空雷。
想見陰宮雪，風門颯踏開。

Heat, no.2

Miasmal clouds never go away.
Lu River again flows from the west.
People behind closed doors lie still.
Birds return to the forest.
In the gorges, everywhere is like fire.
Over the river, after thunders nothing will
    follow.
In the palace of the Hedes, winds noisily
    keep gates open,
For anyone who wants to see snow.

嚴公仲夏枉駕草堂兼攜酒饌 （得寒字）

竹裏行廚洗玉盤，花邊立馬簇金鞍。非關
使者徵求忽，自識將軍禮數寬。百年地闢
柴門迥，五月江深草閣寒。看弄漁舟移白
日，老農何有罄交歡。

In Mid-Summer, Lord Yan Favors me with a Visit to my Thatched Cottage, Bringing Wine and Food (My Allotted Word is "Cold")

Jade pans are washed for the feast among
    bamboos we hold.

Among blooms, your horses stand with
  saddles in gold.
It is not due to the sudden request of your
  messenger,
But the high courtesy to the general I want
  to uphold.
This is always remote with a ramshackle gate.
In June, by a deep river, the thatched cottage
  is cold.
We pass daylight viewing fishing boats in
  action.
What else can be offered for utmost fun by
  a farmer who is old?

石硯

平公今詩伯，秀發吾所羨。奉使三峽中，
長嘯得石硯。巨璞禹鑿餘，異狀君獨見。
其滑乃波濤，其光或雷電。聯坳各盡墨，
多水遞隱現。揮灑容數人，十手可對面。
比公頭上冠，貞質未為賤。當公賦佳句，
況得終清宴。公含起草姿，不遠明光殿。
致于丹青地，知汝隨顧眄。

The Inkstone

Lord Ping, Senior among current poets,
Wins my admiration for his artistry shown.
Sent on a mission in the Three Gorges,
He made a long howl and got an inkstone.
The gentleman alone saw its rarity,
Like the remnant of King Yue's huge uncut
    stone.
Its smoothness takes after billows.
Like thunder and electricity, its light shows.
All joined pits look black
And in deep liquid, come in and out of sight.
Several people can share it with ease,
With ten hands, sitting face to face.
It can compare well with your official hat,
With purity revealing rarity and grace.
It is there when you compose your fine verses,
Not to mention the times for simple leisure,
    all the way.
Your honor is qualified for writing edicts,
Not far is our palace, like Ming Guang Hall
    of yesterday.
Brought to the exalted place, as we know,
You will be looked over by admirers who
    follow.

題郪縣郭三十二明府茅屋壁

江頭且繫船，　為爾獨相憐。雲散灌壇雨，
青春彭澤田。　頻驚適小國，　一擬問高天。
別後巴東路，　逢人問幾賢。

Inscribed on the Wall of a Thatched Cottage of Magistrate Guo, the Thirty-Second, of Qi County

I tied my boat by the river.
For you alone, I develop affinity.
Like Tao Qian, from a minor post since
　　young, you return to the fields.
In your virtuous rule, from rainstorms your
　　county is free.
I often feel shocked you have come to such a
　　small place.
This is something for High Heaven that I
　　want to query.
After parting, on the road of East Ba,
I shall ask everyone I meet who can be as
　　worthy.

玉台觀，其一

中天積翠玉台遙，上帝高居絳節朝。遂有
馮夷來擊鼓，始知嬴女善吹簫。江光隱見
黿鼉窟，石勢參差烏鵲橋。更肯紅顏生羽
翰，便應黃髮老漁樵。

Jade Terrace Temple, no.1

With heaped verdure at mid-sky, Jade
   Terrace Temple is far away.
God presides the court on high, with crimson
   banners in display.
Pingyi, the Water Deity, has come to drum.
Now I know how good at the flute a Ying
   daughter can play.
The river lends me light to see vaguely lairs
   of turtles and crocodiles.
The bridge of magpies span rock formations
   in disarray.
How can I be ruddy-cheeked again and
   productive as a good writer?
I should just age with faded hair and among
   wood-cutters and fishermen stay.

玉台觀, 其二

浩剎因王造，平臺訪古遊。綵雲蕭史駐，
文字魯恭留。宮闕童群帝，乾坤到十州。
人傳有笙鶴，時過北山頭。

Jade Terrace Temple, no. 2

The grand temple was built for a prince.
My visit to the level terrace is for antiquity.
Xiao Shi halted colored clouds with his flute
    music.
Prince Gong of Lu found and kept the words
    of history.
The temple doors lead to the statues of deities.
Paintings of heaven and earth show the Ten
    Isles for immortality.
People say that at times passing the peak to
    the north,
A crane flies, carrying a sheng and a fairy.

春夜喜雨

好雨知時節，當春乃發生。隨風潛入夜，
潤物細無聲。野徑雲俱黑，江船火獨明。
曉看紅溼處，花重錦官城。

Delighting in Rain on a Spring Night

A good rain is aware of seasons.
Spring is right for its onset.
By night, it secretly follows the wind,
Moistening things and keeping small and
  quiet.
Black clouds cover the whole nameless trail.
A lone lit torch is from a boat on the rivulet.
At dawn, watch them in spots that look red
  and wet.

倚杖 （鹽亭縣作）

看花雖郭內，倚杖即溪邊。山縣早休市，
江橋春聚船。狎鷗輕白浪，歸雁喜青天。
物色兼生意，凄涼憶去年。

Leaning on a Cane (Composed at Yanting County)

I am by a creek leaning on a cane,
Watching flowers where town walls enclose.
Boats gather by a bridge of a river in spring.
In this hillside county, markets early close.
Migrating wild geese like blue skies.
Familiar gulls think nothing of billows.

Everything is colorful and lively here.
To the grief rebels caused last year, my
　　thought goes.

遭田父泥飲美嚴中丞

步屧隨春風，村村自花柳。田翁逼社日，
邀我嘗春酒。酒酣誇新尹，畜眼未見有。

迴頭指大男，渠是弓弩手。名在飛騎籍，
長番歲時久。前日放營農，辛苦救衰朽。
差科死則已，誓不舉家走。今年大作社，
拾遺能往否？

叫婦開大瓶，盆中為吾取。感此氣揚揚，
須知風化首。語多雖雜亂，說伊終在口。
朝來偶然出，自卯將及酉。久客惜人情，
如何拒鄰叟。高聲索果栗，欲起時被肘。
指揮過無禮，未覺村野醜。月出遮我留，
仍嗔問升斗。

Made Drunk by an Old Farmer Who Praised Vice Censor-in-chief Yan

My footsteps follow the spring breeze,

118

Past villages with flowers and willows.
An old farmer invites me to take spring ale
When the Festival Day is pressing close.
Fully wined, he praises the new governor.
On scrutiny, someone as good never shows.

Turning his head, he points to his oldest boy:
"He is a master with the crossbows,
With his name on the registers of the cavalry
And seniority in long-term military service.
He was freed for farm work a few days ago,
In hardship to relieve my body on the wane.
Regardless I will pay my taxes until I die
And refuse to take my family to flee.
I shall have a big Spring Festival this year.
For that, can the Reminder stay?"

He calls to his wife to open a big jug of ale
And in a bowl, gives me my share.
Moved by his high energy,
About the prime value of acculturation, I
    now know.
His speech is lengthy and confused.
On the magistrate, he has always something
    to say.

I happen to go out at dawn,
It has been from morning until night.

A long-term stranger, I value good will.
How can I turn a neighbor away?
He asks for fruits and chestnuts aloud.
To stop me from leaving, he uses his elbow.
His orders are too impolite,
But I do not find any peasant-like disgrace.
He still detains me at moonrise,
Taking offence for my asking how much I
have drunk, in my face.

中宵

西閣百尋餘，中宵步綺疏。飛星過水白，
落月動沙虛。擇木知幽鳥，潛波想巨魚。
親朋滿天地，兵甲少來書。

Midnight

West Tower reaches a great height.
I weave my way broadly at midnight.
Sands stay still under the setting moonlight.
A shooting star passing the waters looks
white.
Bird in hiding know about choosing the
right branches.
Big fish submerged under waves want to

be out of sight.
Friends and kin, all over the world,
To me in warfare, seldom write.

不離西閣二首。 其一

江柳非時發，江花冷色頻。地偏應有瘴，
臘近已念春。失學從愚子，無家任老身。
不知西閣意，肯別定留人。

Not Leaving West Tower in Two Poems, no.1

Colorful blooms by the river often open in
    the chill.
Sprouting of riverside willows is untimely.
Near the Laba Festival, there are already
    signs of spring.
Out of miasma, this remote spot should not
    be.
My old body will keep on wandering at will.
From regular schooling, I let my son free.
Who knows of the will of West Tower?
I am not sure if it wants to kick or keep me.

不離西閣二首。 其二

西閣從人別，人今亦故亭。江雲飄素練，
石壁斷空青。滄海先迎口，銀河倒列星。
平生耽勝事，吁駭始初經。

Not Leaving West Tower in Two Poems, no.2

West Tower would not let me leave.
In this old pavilion, I now stay.
Like white silk, clouds above the river float.
By the rocky cliff, a chunk of blue sky seems
　　to break away.
The gray sea is first to receive the sun.
Stars in the Milky Way look inverted in
　　display.
All my life, I indulge myself in scenic spots.
I sigh and get shocked by the new experience
　　today.

數陪李梓州泛江有女樂在諸舫戲為艷曲二
首贈李，其一

上客廻空騎，　佳人滿近船。　江清歌扇底，
野曠舞衣前。　玉袖淩風並，　金壺隱浪偏。
競將明媚色，　偷眼豔陽天

Often Accompanying Li of Zizhou Sailing on the River with Lady Musicians in Several Boats, I Playfully Compose Two Erotic Songs, no.1

The honored guest sends his steed back,
For the boats full of fair ladies nearby.
Before the dancers' robes are the expansive
  wilds.
Under the singers' fans, limpid river waters
  lie.
Golden jugs tilt with hidden waves.
With the wind, jade sleeves seem to fly.
With one another, these dazzling, beguiling
  charmers vie,
Eye-catching under the bright sunlit sky.

數陪李梓州泛江有女樂在諸舫戲為艷曲二
首贈李，其二

白日移歌袖，青霄近笛床。翠眉縈度曲，
雲鬟儼分行。立馬千山暮，廻舟一水香。
使君自有婦，莫學野鴛鴦。

Often Accompanying Li of Zizhou Sailing on the River with Lady Musicians in Several Boats, I Playfully Compose Two Erotic Songs, no.2

The bright sun moves past the singers'
   sleeves.
Near the flutes comes the dark night.
Black knitted brows have corners angled
   upwards.
Their cloud-like temple hair is combed
   neat and tight.
Your returning boat will sail on fragrant
   waters.
Stay your horse for a view of countless hills
   under twilight.
The prefect has his own wife.
Imitating the infidelity of wild mandarin
   ducks is not right.

老病

老病巫山裏，稽留楚客中。藥殘他日裹，
花發去年叢。夜足沾沙雨，春多逆水風。
合分雙賜筆，猶作一飄蓬。

Old and Sick

I am a detained wanderer in Chu,
Old and sick by Wu Hill.
Flowers open from clumps planted last year.
My formerly wrapped medicinal herbs are
    on the wane.
In spring, winds often go against the current.
To wet the sand, there is enough night rain.
I should rid my pair of endowed brushes
Since I am like a rootless tumbleweed still.

戲題寄上漢中王三首，其一

西漢親王子，成都老客星。百年雙白鬢，
一別五秋螢。忍斷杯中物，祇看座右銘。
不能隨皂蓋，自醉逐浮萍。

On Playful Topics, Sent to the Prince of Hanzhong in Three Poems, no.1

You are the Prince of Hanzhong.
In Chengdu, I am a long-term guest.
It has been five years since we part.
On my temples, streaks of white hair rest.
I cannot bear to stop drinking wine.
Only mottos are read instead.
I cannot follow a prefect's carriage with a
　　black awning.
I am just a lone rover with a tipsy head.

戲題寄上漢中王三首，其二

策杖時能出，王門異昔遊。已知嗟不起，
未許醉相當。蜀酒濃無敵，江魚美可求。
終思一酪酊，淨掃雁池頭。

On Playful Topics, Sent to the Prince of Hanzhong in three Poems, no.2

I can often go out with my cane,
But it is a different trip to the prince's gate
　　today.
I already know he only sighs but will not
　　rise.

About detaining me for ale, he has yet to say.
Tasty fish from the river are available.
At the top, strong Shu wine will always stay.
I wish to be drunk in the end
And sweep clean the fish of your pond all the
    way.

戲題寄上漢中王三首，其三

群盜無歸路，　衰顏會遠方。　尚憐詩警策，
猶記酒癲狂。　魯衛彌尊重，　徐陳略喪亡。
空餘枚叟在，　應念早升堂。

On Playful Topics, Sent to the Prince of Hanzhong in Three Poems, no.3

Short of a road home through the rebels,
With an aging face, I meet you far away.
You still recall how I got wild when drunk
And love my poems without spurring
    thoughts to relay.
Like Lu and Wei, the king paid brotherly
    respects to your father.
Like Xu and Chen, in life your clients do not
    stay.
I am a surviving old writer like Mei Sheng in

history.
You should let me in without delay.

九日登梓州城

伊昔黃花酒，如今白髮翁。追歡筋力異，
望遠歲時同。弟妹悲歌裏，朝廷醉眼中。
兵戈與關塞，此日意無窮。

On the Double Ninth Day Climbing the Wall of Zizhou

Right now I am a white-haired man.
I had chrysanthemum wine on a former day.
Our strengths differ in seeking pleasure.
The time of the year is the same for gazing
   far away.
The court comes alive in my drunken eyes.
In my sad songs, memories of my siblings
   stay.
With wars going on near the passes,
My thoughts are endless today.

一室

一室他鄉遠，空林暮景懸。正愁聞塞笛，
獨立見江船。巴蜀來多病，荊蠻去幾年。
應同王粲宅，留井峴山前。

One Cottage

The single cottage is far in a strange land,
With the sun hanging over a deserted grove at
    twilight.
Frontier flutes sadden me just now
As I stand alone, with riverboats in sight.
Since coming to Ba and Shu, I am often sick.
When can I go to Jingzhou, with nomads on
    site?
Wang Chan, a homesick poet, left his house
    and well before Mount Xian.
Both of us should be in the same plight.

棕拂子

棕拂且薄陋，豈知身效能。不堪代白羽，
有足除蒼蠅。熒熒金錯刀，擢擢朱絲繩。
非獨顏色好，亦用顧盼稱。吾老抱疾病，
家貧臥焱蒸。咂膚倦撲滅，賴爾甘服膺。

物微世競棄，義在誰肯徵。三歲清秋至，
未敢缺緘縢。

Palm Whisk

Who would know about the use of a palm
    whisk
That is thin and plain?
Unable to replace white feathers,
It does do just enough so blue flies fail to
    remain.

Like a bright, golden jade-polishing knife,
With a chosen red silk string,
It is also praised for its practical use.
Besides being good looking.

Old and sick,
In my steamy hot cottage, I lie.
Tired of ridding insects that bite,
On its loyalty, I rely.

People rush to trash these humble objects.
Who wants to recruit the just and upright?
Year in year out, when clear fall comes,
I dare not omit storing it all sealed tight.

梅雨

南京犀浦道，　四月熟黃梅。　湛湛長江去，
冥冥細雨來。　茅茨疏易溼。　雲霧密難開。
竟日蛟龍喜，　盤渦與岸廻。

Plum Rain

On Xipu Road, in the south capital,
In the fourth month, ripe plums look yellow.
A drizzle comes in the dark.
Deep and clear, the waters of a long river go.
It is hard for dense clouds and fog to clear
But easy to get wet as gaps of thatches are
　　not narrow.
All day long, joyous flood dragons
Circle by the shore, to and fro.

天池

天池馬不到，　嵐壁鳥繞道。　百頃青雲杪，
曾波白石中。　鬱紆騰秀氣，　蕭瑟浸寒空。
直對巫山峽，　兼疑夏禹功。　魚龍開闢有，
菱芡古今同。　聞道奔雷黑，　初看浴日紅。

飄零神女雨，斷續楚王風。欲問支機石，
如臨獻寶宮。九秋驚雁序，萬里狎漁翁。
更是無人處，誅茅任薄躬。

Pool of Heaven

No horse can reach the pool of Heaven.
Over misty cliffs, only birds can overcome
    the blocks.
A hundred acres in size, at the tip of blue
    clouds,
It has waves in layers among the rocks.

Desolate and lonely, it seems to soak up
    the cold wind.
Luxuriant and elegant, it is an invigorating
    sight.
It faces Mount Wu and the gorges directly.
I also suspect it might be King Yu's
    dredging worksite.

Fish and dragon were here in the creation
    of the world.
Water-chestnuts and caltrops look the same
    as in the past.
For the first time, a red sun bathing in it
    comes in sight.
I have heard it got blackened under thunders

that moved fast.

It receives rain in sprinkles like those for the
    Goddesses of Wu Hill
And gets a good wind, fit for a Chu king.
I want to seek a stone that held up the
    Weaving Maid's loom.
I seem to be approaching a palace with a
    treasure trove for gifting.

In the ninth month in fall, wild geese
    formations may falter.
After myriad miles, familiarity can be
    claimed by a fisherman.
Besides there is a place without inhabitants.
I should seek a thatched cottage here for this
    frail, humble man.

絕句漫興九首，其一

眼見客愁愁不醒，無賴春色到江亭。即遣
花開深造次，便覺鶯語太丁寧。

Rambling Inspirations in Nine Quatrains, no.1

My eyes can tell the wanderer's sorrow in
  me still.
Shamelessly, spring colors reach the riverside
  pavilion against my will.
Even if I dismiss the rash, profuse flowering,
It incites the excessive pitch and frequency
  of the oriole's trill.

絕句漫興九首，其二

手種桃李非無主，野老牆低還是家。恰是
春風相欺得，夜來吹折數枝花。

Rambling Inspirations in Nine Quatrains, no. 2

I planted my own peach and plum trees by
  hand.
With low walls, this is the home of an old
  rustic alright.
The spring wind seems to be bullying us,
Snapping off several floral twigs last night.

絕句漫興九首，其三

熟知茅齋絕低小，江上燕子故來頻。銜泥
點污琴書內，更接飛蟲打著人。

Rambling Inspirations in Nine Quatrains, no.3

Knowing well about my extremely low and
    small thatched study,
Swallows above the river on purpose fly in
    again and again.
Besides catching flying insects and bumping
    up against me,
In my books and qin, from their beaks they
    leave many a mud stain.

絕句漫興九首，其四

二月已破三月來，漸老逢春幾能回。莫思
身外無窮事，且盡生前有限杯。

Rambling Inspirations in Nine Quatrains, no. 4

The second month is over; the third month is

to unfold.

How many more springs can I face alone,
getting old?

Mind not the endless impersonal affairs.

Before death, rather empty the limited cups of
wine one can hold.

絕句漫興九首，其五

腸斷春江欲盡頭，杖藜徐步立芳州。癲狂
柳絮隨風舞，輕薄桃花逐水流。

Rambling Inspirations in Nine Quatrains, no.5

Heartbroken by the river, as spring is about
to be spent,

I stroll with my cane and stand on an isle with
a fragrant floral scent.

Willow fluff madly follows the wind.

Light, thin peach petals chase the water
current.

絕句漫興九首，其六

懶慢無堪不出村，呼兒日在掩柴門。蒼苔
濁酒林中靜，碧水春風野外暮。

Rambling Inspirations in Nine Quatrains, no.6

Unbearably lazy and slow, in my village I
　　stay,
Asking my son to shut my ramshackle gate
　　all day.
In the quiet grove, with dark green moss and
　　unfiltered wine,
I have blue waters and spring breeze until
　　dusk, all the way.

絕句漫興九首，其七

糝徑楊花鋪白氈，點溪荷葉疊青錢。筍根
雉子無人見，沙上鳧雛傍母眠。

Rambling Inspirations in Nine Quatrains, no.7

Like a white rug on the path, willow fluff

makes a cover.

Like green coins in a creek, lotus leaves
stack on one another.

Nobody sees the pheasant chicks by bamboo
roots.

On the sand, wild ducklings sleep by their
mother.

絕句漫興九首，其八

舍西柔桑葉可拈，江畔細麥復纖纖。人生
幾何春已夏，不放香醪如蜜甜。

Rambling Inspirations in Nine Quatrains, no.8

West of my cottage, mulberry leaves for
picking look tender.

Riverside wheat also looks tiny and slender.

How long is my life, now that spring has
become summer?

Fragrant wine, sweet like honey, is not for
me to surrender.

絕句漫興九首，其九

隔戶楊柳弱嫋嫋，恰似十五女兒腰。誰謂
朝來不作意，狂風挽斷最長條。

Rambling Inspirations in Nine Quatrains, no.9

The willow next door looks graceful and
    lean,
Just like a girl's waist at fifteen.
A wild blast broke the longest branch.
Who would be mindful enough at dawn,
    sight unforeseen?

贈王二十四侍禦契四十韻

I

往往雖相見，飄飄愧此身。不關輕絖冕，
俱是避風塵。一別星橋夜，三移斗柄春。
敗亡非赤壁，奔走為黃巾。子去何瀟灑，
予藏異隱淪。書成無過雁，衣故有懸鶉。
恐懼行裝數，伶俜臥疾頻。曉鶯工迸淚，

139

秋月解傷神。會面嗟鬚黑，含淒話苦辛。
接輿還入楚，王粲不歸秦。

II

錦里殘丹竈，花溪得釣綸。消中祇自惜，
晚起索誰親。伏柱聞周史，乘槎有漢臣。
鵷鴻不易狎，龍虎未宜馴。客則掛冠至，
交非傾蓋新。由來意氣合，直取性情真。
浪跡同生死，無心恥賤貧。偶然存蔗芋，
幸各對松筠。糲飯依他日，窮愁怪此辰。
女長裁褐穩，男大卷書勻。

III

灊口江如練，鹽崖雪似銀。名園當翠巘，
野棟沒青蘋。屢喜王侯宅，時邀江海人。
追隨不覺晚，款曲動彌旬。但使芝蘭秀，
何煩棟宇鄰。山陽無俗物，鄭驛正留賓。
出入並鞍馬，光輝參席珍。重遊先主廟，
更歷少城闉。石鏡通幽魄，琴臺隱絳脣。
送終惟糞土，結愛獨荊榛。

IV

置酒高林下，　觀棋積水濱。　區區甘累趼，
稍稍息勞筋。　網聚粘圓鯽，　絲繁煮細蓴。
長歌敲柳癭，　小睡憑籐輪。　農月須知課，
田家敢忘勤。　浮生難去食，　良會惜清晨。
列國兵戈暗，　今王德教淳。　要聞除猰㺄。
休作畫麒麟。　洗眼看輕薄，　虛懷任屈伸。
莫令膠漆地，　萬古重雷陳。

Presented to Attendant Censor Wang Qi, the Twenty-Fourth, in Forty Couplets

I

Though I meet you often,
I am ashamed of being swept here and there.
With no slight to a high government post,
I hide from the wind and dust of warfare.

Once we parted that night on Seven Star
　Bridge,
Thrice the Dipper's Handle has shifted to
　spring.
The defeat was not total, like that at the
　Red Cliff,
But the local rebels, like the Yellow Turbans,

141

kept us running.

How relaxed you were when you left.
From that of a hermit, my hiding was
    different.
My old robes wear down with patches.
Without passing wild geese, my letters
    cannot be sent.

More than once, I packed my luggage
    in fear.
Wandering alone, I often lie in disease.
The fall moon soothes my worn spirit.
Dawn orioles bring me tears with ease.

Those I meet sigh over my tanned look.
I talk about my hardship with grief.
Like Jieyu returning to Chu, I go back to
    Chengdu.
Like Wang Can fleeing from Changsha, I
    hold the same belief.

II

At Washing Flower Creek, I found my
    fishing line.
In Chengdu, my stove for elixirs is in an
    inactive state.

I pity myself for being diabetic.
Whom do I seek after rising late?

Like the Zhou archivist and the Han officer
    on a raft,
You are as acclaimed.
It is neither easy to be casual with fellow
    ministers
Nor proper to get the hard-nosed ones tamed.

I am a guest here, having quit my office.
Our close friendship is not new.
Our temperaments have always coincided,
With our mutual appreciation of ingenuity
    coming through.

I care not about my low status and poverty.
In my wanderings, life and death mean the
    same to me.
By chance, I have in store my sugarcane and
    taro.
With luck, we can have pine and bamboo for
    company.

Coarse meals will be mine in future.
Poor and worried, I feel strange.
My grown daughter makes homespun robes
    with steady hands.

To roll the scrolls in an even manner, my big
    son can arrange.

III

At Pengkou, the river is like silk.
Like silver, Can cliff has snow.
Famous gardens face verdant mountains.
Into green duckweeds, my coarse oars go.

I always enjoy your grand mansion.
You have often invited this wanderer out
    on river and sea.
Being with you makes me oblivious to time.
A stay of ten days is fast in your hospitality.

If only lingzhis and orchids flourish,
Why worry about our living close?
Like Zheng's lodge, your house has a guest
    retained.
Like Shanyang, nothing mundane and
    worldly shows.

In and out, side by side, we go on horseback.
We are treasured for our shining scholarship
    and Confucian value.
Again we visit the temple of the first king,
    Liu Bei

And to the "Little City", find the gate to pass
　　through.

"Stone Mirror" is the portal to the tomb of
　　a consort.
The crimson lips of the wife of Sima Xiangru
　　were buried at "Zither Terrace".
Their lives ended with dung and soil.
Only brambles and bushes entwine their
　　lovers in embrace.

IV

We set out wine under tall trees
And by the waters, watch a chess game.
My tired sinews can take a short rest.
I am willing to burden my calloused feet,
　　with no claim to fame.

We boil fine water-shields with many
　　filaments.
Netted carps get rounded and stuck without
　　a gap.
We sing for long, tapping on the gall of a
　　willow.
Coils of vines make bedding for a short nap.

In the farming months, one needs to be aware

of the tasks.
Farmers dare not forget about hard work.
In a drifting life, it is difficult to be hungry.
I value this fine gathering, early in the day.

The present king holds a kind, virtuous reign.
Warfare darkens various states.
I would like to hear about efforts to rid rebels.
At the palace Hall of Fame, stop painting
  portraits.

My eyes are clear on pettiness.
To life's ups and downs, I am open-minded.
On our land that values friendship bonded
  like glue,
Do not just let Lei and Chen, historical good
  friends, to be reminded.

奉漢中王手劄報韋侍禦蕭尊師亡

秋日蕭韋逝，淮王報峽中。少年疑柱史，
多術怪仙公。不但時人惜，祇應吾道窮。
一衰侵疾病，相識自兒童。處處鄰家笛，
飄飄客子蓬。強吟懷舊賦，已作白頭翁。

On Receiving a Letter from the Prince of Hanzhong, Informing me of the Death of Attendant Censor Wei and Reverend Xiao

Xiao and Wei passed on in autumn.
In the gorges, I got this from the Prince to
    share.
The many skills of the Daoist priest in the
    occult art marvels me.
The young censor could not have died in such
    an early year.
Not only do their contemporaries feel sorry.
Of my blocked path in life, I am aware.
I knew them since childhood.
Sadly, illnesses bring me wear and tear.
Like a tumbleweed, I am a wanderer adrift,
Hearing flute music on late friends from
    neighborhoods everywhere.
Forcing myself to chant poems in memory
    of dead friends,
I am already an elder with white hair.

奉寄高常侍

汶上相逢年頗多，飛騰無那故人何。總戎
楚蜀應全未，方駕曹劉不啻過。今日朝廷

147

須汲黯，中原將帥憶廉頗。天涯春色催遲暮，別淚遙添錦水波。

Respectfully Sent to Attendant Gao

Since we met by River Wen, it has been
    many a year.
With my old friend's soaring success, how
    can I compare?
You have yet to be in full control of forces
    in Chu and Shu,
But overtaken poets Cao Zhi and Liu Zhen,
    in a pair.
Today, the court needs direct remonstrators
    like Ji An.
Commanders on the Central Plain recall
    Lian Po, a top strategist in warfare.
Afar my parting tears add to the waves of
    Brocade River.
My old age speeds up with another round of
    spring colors everywhere.

奉寄章十侍禦

淮海維揚一俊人，金章紫綬照青春。指麾
能事迴天地，訓練強兵動鬼神。湘西不得

148

歸關羽，河內猶宜借寇恂。朝覲從容問幽
仄，勿云江漢有垂綸。

Respectfully Sent to Censor Zhang, the Tenth

This smart man shines in green spring, from
Yangzhou to Huaihai.
Gold seals and purple sashes are what he gets
to wear.
His well-trained, strong army can shock
spirits and deities.
His efficient leadership can twist Heaven
and Earth everywhere.
West of Xiang, one could not bring back
GuanYu,
But in Henei, it was alright to borrow Kou
Xun as governor for another year.
At ease in the dawn court, if the king asks
about recluses,
Do not say by River Han, another hermit like
me is fishing there.

送竇九歸成都

文章亦不盡，竇子才縱橫。非爾更苦節，
何人符大名。讀書雲閣觀，問絹錦官城。
我有浣花竹，題詩須一行。

Seeing off Dou, the Ninth, on his Return to Chengdu

Master Dou's talent is peerless.
Your literary output is in an endless flow.
Without your harder push with grit,
Who could live up to such great renown.
You studied at the Cloud Pavilion Temple.
To visit your father at Chengdu, you will go.
I have bamboos like those of Washing
  Flower Creek.
For a visit to write poems, you need to come
  down.

送嚴侍郎到棉州同登杜使君江樓（得心字）

野興每難盡，江樓延賞心。歸朝送使節，
落景惜登臨。稍稍煙集渚，微微風動襟。
重船依淺瀨，輕鳥度層陰。襜峻背幽谷，

窗虛交茂林。燈光散遠近，月彩靜高深。
城擁朝來客，天橫醉後參。窮途衰謝意，
苦調短長吟。此會共能幾，諸孫賢至今。
不勞朱戶閉，自待白河沉。

Seeing off Vice-Director Yan at Mianzhou as we Climb together to the Upper Story of the Riverside Mansion of Prefect Du (my Allotted Word is 'Heart')

Enjoying nature can never be complete.
At the riverside tower, more joy to the
 heart can go.
In seeing off the commissioner for his return
 to the court,
We value climbing to see sunset aglow.
Thin mist gathers on the isles.
Our lapels flap as faint winds blow.
A huge boat is at the shoals.
Light birds pass the layered shadow.
A secluded valley lies behind a high railing.
A dense forest with crossed twigs lends its
 view through my open window.
Light from lanterns spreads far and near.
Quietly, high and remote is the moon-glow.
Morning visitors visit the city.
After we are drunk, Heaven lets the mass of
 constellation Orion show.

At the roadblock of my life, my creativity is
on the wane.
My long and short poems touch on sorrow.
My grand nephew Du is always a sage prefect.
How many more gatherings like this can
follow?
Do not bother to close your red door to detain
your guests.
I shall wait to see the bright Milky Way sink
and lose its glow.

投簡梓州幕府兼簡韋十郎官

幕下郎官安穩無，從來不奉一行書。固知
貧病人須棄，能使韋郎跡也疏。

Sent as a Note to the Zizhou Headquarters and to Director Wei, the Tenth

Are the gentlemen in the headquarters fine?
You never sent me a letter of even one line.
I surely know that people should shun the
poor and sick
And why few tracks of Director Wei meet
mine.

寄韋有夏郎中

省郎憂病士， 書信有柴胡。 飲子頻通汗，
懷君想報珠。 親知天畔少， 藥味峽中無。
歸楫生衣臥， 春鷗洗翅呼。 猶聞上急水，
早作取平途。 萬里皇華使， 為僚記腐儒。

Sent to Director Wei Youxia

The divisional director sent me a medicinal
   herb, chai hu, in the mail,
Worried about a sick man like me.
I think of repaying him with a pearl as a gift.
I sweat often after drinking the herbal tea.

Close friends are few at the sky's edge.
In the gorges, this medicine cannot be found.
My returning boat has oars lain in moss.
In spring, gulls bathe their wings and make
   sound.

I heard you were sailing near rapids.
Take the level road early on your way.
As a friend, think of me, a rotten, useless
   scholar.
You are the king's brilliant envoy, endless
   miles away.

153

不寐

瞿塘夜水黑，城內改更籌。翳翳月沉霧，
煇煇星近樓。氣衰甘少寐，心弱恨知愁。
多壘滿山谷，桃源無處求。

Sleepless

At night, the waters of Qutang are black.
City watch clappers sound for a different
    hour.
Dimly the moon sinks within a fog.
Bright stars draw near to a tower.
With waned energy, I am fine with little sleep.
I hate sad news when my heart lacks power.
Many forts fill the hills and valleys, blocking
    my search
For the paradise by a stream with many a
    peach flower.

李潮八分小篆歌

倉頡鳥跡既茫昧，字體變化如浮雲。陳倉
石鼓又已訛，大小二篆生八分。秦有李斯
漢蔡邕，中間作者絕不聞。嶧山之碑野火
焚，棗木傳刻肥失真。苦縣光和尚骨立，

154

書貴瘦硬方通神。惜哉李蔡不復得，吾甥
李潮下筆親。尚書韓擇木，騎曹蔡有鄰。
開元已來數八分，潮也奄有子成三人。況
潮小篆逼秦相，快劍長戟森相向。八分一
字直百金，蛟龍盤拏肉屈強。吳郡張顛跨
草書，草書非古空雄壯。豈如吾甥不流
宕，丞相中郎丈人行。巴東逢李潮，逾月
求我歌。我今衰老才力薄，潮乎潮乎奈汝
何。

Song for Li Chao's Bafen Small Seal Script

We are ignorant of Cang Jie's words based
   on birds' claw prints.
Like drifting clouds, changed forms of
   characters may be indescript.
Even carvings on stone drums at Chencang
   may be wrong.
After the big and small Seal Scripts came the
   Bafen Script.

Between Li Si of Qin and Cai Yong of Han,
No other famous calligraphers were known.
Wildfires wrecked the stele at Mount Yi.
Carvings on date wood look unreal as the
   size is too full-blown.

Ku County's stele of the Guanghe reign
    still stands.
A script is valued for thin and stiff lines,
    hence more lively as such.
It is regrettable the works of Li and Cai did
    not last.
My nephew, Li Chao, moves his brush with
    a human touch.

Han Zemu of the Secretariat
And Cai Youlin of the Horse Guard
Recognized the Bafen Script in the Kaiyuan
    reign.
Besides these two, on his own, the rank of the
    Third Master Chao can gain.

What is more, Chao's Small Seal Script
    presses close to that of the Qin minister.
Like packed fast swords and long pikes,
    brush strokes are set face to face.
A single character of his in the Bafen Script
    is worth a thousand in gold.
Like a coiled flood dragon with strong
    muscular grips, compactness is in place.

Crazy Zhang of Wu County brag of his Draft
    Script.
But the Draft Script is done with power in

vain, with no link to the past.
With the Minister and Court Gentlemen,
  Chao walks with mature propriety.
How can the calligraphy of my nephew,
  without lax fluidity, be surpassed?

I met Li Chao at East Ba.
He asked a song of me and a month is
  through.
Now I have waned in health and talent.
Chao, O Chao! What can I do for you?

傷春五首，其一

天下兵雖滿，春光日自濃。西京疲百戰，
北闕任群凶。關塞三千里，煙花一萬重。
蒙塵清路急，禦宿且誰供。殷復前王道，
周遷舊國容。蓬萊足雲氣，應合總從龍。

Spring Lament in Five Poems, no.1

Though soldiers are packed everywhere,
Spring sunlight is intense by day.
Changan is worn out by a hundred battles.
Fearsome mobs at the palace are left to make

a foray.

The frontier is myriad miles away.
Endless layers of misty blooms pile high.
In haste, the king fled the capital.
For lodging, on whom could he rely?

The way of former Yin kings was restored.
To a new capital elsewhere, A Zhou emperor
    had to go.
Enough auspicious clouds above Penglai
    palace
Should be fit for dragons, a symbol of
    kingship, to follow.

傷春五首，其二

鶯入新年語，花開滿故枝。天青同卷幔，
草碧水通池。牢落官軍速，蕭條萬事危。
鬢毛元自白，淚點向來垂。不是無兄弟，
其如有別離。巴山春已靜，北望轉逶迤。

Spring Lament in Five Poems, no.2

New Year begins with the orioles' trill.
On old twigs, the full glory of blooming

displays.

Drapes roll in the wind under the blue sky.

Water reaches a pool near green grass on
waterways.

Scarce and scattered, royal troops are in haste.

In a desolate and dangerous state, everything
stays.

My temple hair is already white.

Teardrops are falling always.

It is not that I lack brothers,

But separations make me feel the same in
ways.

Colors of Mount Ba in spring are subtle.

At the distant north, I turn to gaze.

傷春五首，其三

日月還相鬥，星辰屢合圍。不成誅執法，
焉得變危機。大角纏兵氣，鉤陳出帝畿。
煙塵昏禦道，耆舊把天衣。行在諸軍闕，
來朝大將稀。賢多隱屠釣，王肯載同歸。

Spring Lament in Five Poems, no.3

The sun and the moon still vie.

Evil omens from stars we often get to share.

How can we turn dangers around,
If the lives of hired assassins in the name of
    law are for us to spare?
As the king flees, the Gouchen star leaves the
    royal domain.
The Great Horn Constellation foretells
    warfare.
Smoke and dust dim the imperial highway.
Old people fondly touch the robes the king
    used to wear.
Many armies are missing in the war capital.
High generals joining the new court are rare.
Worthies mostly hide as butchers and
    fishermen.
Will the king recruit one and return in a pair?

傷春五首，其四

再有朝廷亂，難知消息真。近傳王在洛，
復道使歸秦。奪馬悲公主，登車泣貴嬪。
蕭關迷北上，滄海欲東巡。敢料安危體，
猶多老大臣。豈無嵇紹血，沾灑屬車塵。

Spring Lament in Five Poems, no.4

Once more, the court faces unrest.

It is hard to know if the information is true.
Lately, there is word the king is at Luoyang.
An official was sent to Changan, from other
    words that came through.
Noble consorts wept as a Jin king surrendered
    his palace.
A princess grieved with her horse taken by a
    rebel in history.
At Xiao Pass, a Han monarch got lost in a
    northern expedition.
The first Qin emperor wanted to reach the sun,
    east of the gray sea.
I dare not predict on our national security.
There are still many old, senior ministers.
Ji Shao got killed and saved a Jin king's life.
His blood in a spray got mixed with the dust
    of the royal carriage.

傷春五首，其五

聞說初東華， 孤兒卻走多。 難分太倉粟，
競棄魯陽戈。 胡虜登前殿， 王公出禦河。
得無中夜舞， 誰憶大風歌。 春色生烽燧，
幽人泣薜蘿。 君臣重修德， 猶足見時和。

Spring Lament in Five Poems, no.5

Many imperial guards, called "orphans", ran
off
When the king first fled east, from hearsay.
Without a share of the grains from the royal
granary,
They raced to desert the army, with morale
in decay.
When nomad rebels mounted the front palace,
On the imperial boat, princes and dukes
sailed away.
Do we not have people like Jin fighters who
practiced the sword dance at midnight?
Who recalls "The Big Wind Song" when we
lack soldiers in the same way?
A recluse weeps in his hermit's robe.
Beacon fires appear amid colors of nature on
a spring day.
If the ruler and commoners value fostering
morals again,
It is enough to let us see peace here to stay.

峽中覽物

曾為掾吏趨三輔，憶在潼關詩興多。巫峽
忽如瞻華嶽，蜀江猶似見黃河。舟中得病

移衾枕，洞口經春長薜蘿。形勝有餘風土
惡，幾時回首一高歌。

Taking in the Sights of the Gorges

Once a secretary for three chiefs,
I recall at Tong Pass how my poetic
   inspiration reached a height.
Suddenly, Wu Gorge looks like Mount Hua.
Yangzi in Shu is Yellow River to my sight.
Creepers lengthen in spring at the mouths
   of caves.
Sick in my boat, I move my quilt and pillow.
When can I return home and sing high?
The scenery here is superb, but customs are
   base and low.

武侯廟

遺廟丹青落，空山草木長。獨聞辭後主，
不復臥南陽。

The Temple of Zhuge Liang

Colored temple murals crumble and fall.
On deserted hills, grass and trees grow tall.

I can still hear what the minister of war said
    to the orphan king.
Rather than returning to Nanyang, he would
    stay on for his call.

因崔五侍禦寄高彭州適一絕

百年已過半，秋至轉飢寒。為問彭州牧，
何時救急難？

Through Vice-Censor Cui, the Fifth, I Send a Quatrain to Gao Shi of Pengzhou

I have already passed half of my life
In fall, hungry and cold I shall be.
Let me ask the official of Pengzhou:
When can you rescue me from an emergency?

寄彭州高三十五使君適虢州岑二十七長史參三十韻

I

故人何寂寞，今我獨淒涼。老去才雖盡，
秋來興甚長。物情尤可見，辭客未能忘。
海內知名士，雲端各異方。高岑殊緩步，
沈鮑得同行。意愜關飛動，篇終接混茫。
舉天悲富駱，近代惜盧王。似爾官仍貴，
前賢銘可傷。諸侯非棄擲，半刺已翱翔。
詩好幾時見，書成無信將。

II

男兒行處是，客子鬥身強。羈旅推賢聖，
沉綿抵咎殃。三年猶瘧疾，一鬼不銷亡。
隔日搜脂髓，增寒抱雪霜。徒然潛隙地，
有靦屢鮮妝。何太龍鍾極，于今出處妨。
無錢居帝里，盡室在邊疆。劉表雖遺恨，
龐公至死藏。心微傍魚鳥，肉瘦怯豺狼。
隴草蕭蕭白，洮雲片片黃。

165

III

彭門劍閣外，虢略鼎湖旁。荊玉簪頭冷，
巴箋染翰光。烏麻蒸續曬，丹橘露應嘗。
豈異神仙宅，俱兼山水鄉。竹齋燒藥竈，
花嶼讀書床。更得清新否，遙知對屬忙。
舊官寧改漢，淳俗本歸唐。濟世宜公等，
安貧亦士常。蚩尤終戮辱，胡羯漫猖狂。
會待妖氛靜，論文暫裹糧。

To Gao Shi, the Thirty-Fifth, Prefect of Pengzhou and Cen Shen, the Twenty-Seventh, Aide in Guizhou: Thirty Couplets

I

How quiet my old friends can be
To make me sad being alone!
Though my talent ends as I age,
In fall, much inspiration has grown.

I can see how things go.
These poets cannot fade from my memory.
Living at different edges of clouds,
They are famous on this land by the sea.

Bao Zao and Shan Yue had similar prosodic

skills.
The lines of Gao Shi and Cen Shen shared the
    same relaxed glow.
In the right mood, their creativity takes wing.
To the height of the primordial chaos, their
    finished poems can go.

The whole world grieves over the passing of
    Fu Jiamo and Luo Binwang.
Regrettable is the loss of Lu Zhaolin and
    Wang Bo of late.
You gentlemen are holding prized posts
While ancient worthies met their sad fate.

Prefects, like regional lords, are not trash.
Aides, like half a prefect, have already soared
    in flight.
When can I read your fine poems?
I finished my letter, without a messenger in
    sight.

II

A true man accepts wherever he may go.
A traveler fights to keep his body strong.
I promote wise men's teachings as a detained
    wanderer.
Bogged down by sickness, I resist blame and

mishaps all along.

For three years, I am still down with malaria.
The ghost-like disease has not gone away.
Embraced by snow and frost with more chill,
My fat and marrow get sapped every other
    day.

I often put fresh make-up on my uneasy face,
Hiding on an empty lot in vain.
Why am I looking so aged now,
Stuck between wanting to leave or remain?

Penniless, I live in the capital.
My whole household is here in the frontier.
Liu Biao regretted he failed to recruit Pang
    Degong,
A military strategist and hermit who, until
    death, did not appear.

With a thin body, I am timid before wolves
    and jackals.
I keep fish and birds company as my mood is
    mellow.
In the whistling wind, Longyou's grass looks
    bleached.
All clouds above River Tao turn yellow.

III

Mount Pengmen lies beyond Sword Pavilion.
Guolue stands beside Lake Ding.
Hairpins made of Mount Jing's jade feel cold.
On the paper of Ba, there is a glow from
    ink-and-brush writing.

You can steam and dry black sesame seeds
And should drink red tangerine juice like dew.
Not different from those of fairies,
Your house, by hill and river, commands a
    view.

Your bamboo study has a stove to boil
    medicine.
Your couch for reading is an islet for minds
    like flowers to grow.
Have you made new, refreshing verses?
You are busy on antithetical couplets, from
    afar I know.

Your old office has not shun Han practices.
Folk customs take origin from Tang ways.
To save the world is fitting for you gentlemen.
Poor scholars are contented in every case.

Like Chiyou, An Lushan will finally meet

his insult and death.
Hu and Jie nomads are too unruly and heady.
We shall wait for the demonic energy to end.
Meanwhile, for our talks on literature, I shall
have my provisions ready.

存歿口號二首，其一

席謙不見近彈棋，畢耀仍傳舊小詩。玉局
他年無限笑，白楊今日幾人悲。

Two Extempore Poems on the Living and the Dead, no.1

We do not see Xi Qian, an expert chess
player of a former day.
They still circulate the short poems of Bi Yao,
left from yesterday.
Some year, at jade chessboards, peals of
laughter may be endless.
By white poplars of graveyards, how many
people grieve today?

存歿口號二首，其二

鄭公粉繪隨長夜，曹霸丹青已白頭。天下
何曾有山水，人間不解重驊騮。

Two Extempore Poems on the Living and the Dead, no.2

Zheng Qian, good at colored paintings, has
    been underground each long night.
Cao Ba painted with pigments, but his hair is
    already white.
When did this world ever have such fine
    landscapes?
Earthlings bypass rare steeds due to oversight.

引水

月峽瞿塘雲作頂，亂石崢嶸俗無井。雲安
沽水奴僕悲，漁復移居心力省。白帝城西
萬竹蟠，接筒因引水喉不乾。人生留滯生
理難，斗水何直百憂寬。

Water Conduits

All-cloudy Qutang Gorge is moonlit bright.

Wells are by custom absent; jumbled rocks
   reach a height.
After moving to live in Yufu County, I have
   less hassle.
Buying water at Yunan County, my servants
   are in a sad plight.

Endless bamboos wind White Emperor
   Fortress to the west.
By life's problems, a detained wanderer is
   hard pressed.
My throat is not dry, with water through
   conduits of bamboo.
How can a ladle of water put my hundred
   worries to rest?

Year 765-767

課伐木

I

長夏無所為，客居課好僕。清晨飯其腹，
持斧入白谷。青冥曾巔後，十里斬陰木。

人肩四根已，　亭午下山麓。　尚聞丁丁聲，
功課日各足。　蒼皮成積委，　素節相照燭。
藉汝跨小籬，　當仗苦虛竹。　空荒咆熊羆，
乳獸待人肉。　不示知禁情，　豈惟干戈哭。
城中賢府主，　處貴如白屋。

II

蕭蕭理體淨，　蜂蠆不敢毒。　虎穴連里閭，
陧防舊風俗。　泊舟滄江岸，　久客慎所觸。
舍西岸嶠壯，　雷雨蔚含蓄。　牆宇資屢修，
衰年怯幽獨。　爾曹輕執熱，　為我忍煩促。
秋光近青岑，　季月當泛菊。　報之以微寒，
共給酒一斛。

Assigning the Task of Tree Cutting

I

This long summer, with nothing to do,
I assigned my servants a task, as a guest
　resident.
After having rice in early morning,
Into White Valley, holding axes they went.

Under the dark blue sky, past layer ridges,

For ten miles, they cut trees on the north
    hillside.
At noon, they stopped and came down.
The rule of each shouldering four trunks was
    applied.

To them, the sound of tree cutting still rang.
The task for each was well done every day.
The dark gray bark became a pile.
White bare stems shone like candles in a way.

I rely on these to join tiny hedges,
As hollow bamboos as barriers lack weight.
Bears roar in the empty wilds.
For human flesh, nursing cubs are in wait.

If I did not show my concern of this taboo,
I would be weeping for wars alone.
In the city, a sage chief commander
Ranks my thatched cottage as high as his own.

II

He solemnly manages a clean government.
To sting like wasps and scorpions, criminals
    do not dare.
Tigers' lairs are close to our neighborhoods.
It is an old custom here to beware.

I moored my boat by the shore of a gray river.
What I come across, I heed, being a stranger
  for a long time here.
West of my cottage, lush vegetations cover
  cliffs and ridges.
In a rainstorm, the exuberance is not clear.

My walls and roof need frequent repairs.
As I age, I fear isolation and quietness.
You all do not mind the persistent heat
And for my sake, put up with this onerous
  task no less.

Autumn lights are close to green ridges.
In the last month of fall, attention on
  chrysanthemums should be spent.
Let the big pot of wine from me
And the coming light chill be the repayment.

曉望白帝城鹽山

徐步移班杖，看山仰白頭。翠深開斷壁，
紅遠結飛樓。日出清江望，暄和散旅愁。
春城見松雪，始擬進歸舟。

175

At Dawn, Watching Salt Hill from White Emperor Fortress

I raise my white-haired head to watch the hill.
My walk with a mottled cane is slow.
Red eaves of the distant tower seem to fly.
The verdancy of steep cliffs begins to show.
As I look out by a clear stream at sunrise,
The warmth eases the wanderer's sorrow.
At the fortress in spring, I see pines in snow.
Then to the returning boat, I start to go.

公安送李二十九弟晉肅入蜀予下沔鄂

正解柴桑纜，仍看蜀道行。檣烏相背發，
塞雁一行鳴。南紀連銅柱，西江接錦城。
憑將百錢卜，漂泊問君平。

At Gongan, Seeing off Cousin Li Jinsu, the Twenty Ninth Going to Shu, before my Departure for Mianzhou and Ezhou

I fix my gaze at your walk on the road to Shu
When at Chaisang, for my boat I undo the tie.
Crows on my mast leave by opposite routes.
In one line, frontier wild geese cry.
West River conjoins Brocade City.

Near the Southern Boundary, remnants of a
　bronze column lie.
To divine my luck at Junping's store in
　Chengdu,
On you, this wanderer will rely.

最能行

峽中丈夫絕輕死，少在公門多在水。富豪
有錢駕大舸，貧窮取給行艇子。小兒學問
止論語，大兒結束隨商旅。欹帆側柁入波
濤，撇漩捎濆無險阻。朝發白帝暮江陵，
傾來目擊信有徵。瞿塘漫天虎鬚怒，歸州
長年行最能。此鄉之人氣量窄，誤競南風
疏北客。若道士無英俊才，何得山有屈原
宅。

Ballad of the Most Capable

In the gorges, men think nothing of death.
More on waters than in offices, they strive.
The rich and powerful sail large boats.
In small sampans, the poor make their deals
　in life.

Small children are taught the analects only.

Behind traveling merchants, big boys get
  packed and follow.
Oblivious to danger, they swerve past
  whirlpools and surges.
With sails and rudders aslant, they get into
  many a billow.

Leaving White Emperor Fortress at dawn,
  they reach Jiangling at night.
For credibility, I have recent eyewitness
  reports to go by.
Old timers of Guizhou have the best skill.
Like angry roaring tigers, torrents at Qutang
  Gorge are sky high.

People of this area, narrow minded and aloof
  to northerners,
Vie to mimic southern manners by mistake.
If you think there is a lack of brilliance here,
Of the hillside house of Qu Yuan, what do
  you make?

卜居

歸羨遼東鶴，吟同楚執珪。未成遊碧海，
著處覓丹梯。雲障覓江北，春耕破瀼西。
桃紅客若至，定似昔人迷。

Choosing my Residence

Like the Chu official, I prefer to moan in
　　my dialect.
I envy the man from Liaodong returning
　　home as a crane.
I seek a cinnabar ladder everywhere to
　　reach the immortals.
Touring the fairies' Sapphire Sea is in vain.
The soil of west of the river is broken up
　　for spring cultivation.
Blocked by clouds, a view of north of the
　　stream I cannot gain.
Should a visitor come as peach flowers
　　turn pink here,
He would be another man astray in utopia,
　　yearning to remain.

同元使君（舂陵行）并序

序： 覽道州元使君結（舂陵行）兼（賊退後示官吏作）二首，志之曰：當天子分憂之地，効漢朝良吏之日。今盜賊未息，知民疾苦，得結輩十數公，落落然參錯天下為邦伯，萬物吐氣，天下小安可待矣！不意復見比興體制，微婉頓挫之詞，感而有詩，增諸卷軸，簡知我者，不必寄元。

I

遭亂髮盡白， 轉衰病相嬰。沉綿盜賊際，
狼狽江漢行。歎時藥力薄，為客贏瘵成。
吾人詩家秀，博采世上名。粲粲元道州，
前聖畏後生。觀乎（舂陵）作，歘見俊哲
情。復覽（賊退）篇，結也實國楨。賈誼
昔流慟，匡衡嘗引經。道州憂黎庶，詞氣
浩縱橫。兩章對秋月，一字偕華星。致君
唐虞際，淳朴憶大庭。何時降璽書，用爾
為丹青。

II

獄訟永衰息，豈惟偃甲兵！淒惻念誅求，
薄斂近休明。乃知正人意，不苟飛長纓。

180

涼飆振南嶽，之子寵若驚。色沮金印大，
興含滄浪清。我多長卿病，日久思朝廷。
肺枯渴太甚，漂泊公孫城。呼兒具紙筆，
隱几臨軒楹。作詩呻吟內，墨淡字敧傾。
感彼危苦詞，庶幾知者聽。

A Companion Piece to the Poem "Ballad of Chongling" by Prefect Yuan, with a Preface

Preface: After reading two poems of Yuan Jie, Prefect of Daozhou: "Ballad of Chongling" and "Addressed to my Officials and Subordinates, after the Retreat of Rebels", I have a comment. Wherever Yuan is assigned by the Son of Heaven to share his worries about regional problems, he fits the rank of good officials by Han Dynasty standards.

Now rebels are still active. The trouble and pain of commoners are well known. If we could get a dozen or more men like Yuan and send them to different parts of our country as exceptional governors, everything would revive. The first step leading to national stability could be hoped for.

Out of my expectation, I again see verses by
Yuan expressed in metaphors and
associations which are melodious and smooth.
Moved, I wrote a poem to add to his book. I
send this note to those who understand me,
not necessarily for Yuan.

I

At war, my hair all turned white.
My waning body is trapped in disease.
Sunk in ill health, with rebels rampant,
I wander on rivers, ill at ease.

I sigh for the times; my medicine is of
    little use.
As a wanderer, I got weak since illnesses
    came.
I stand out among poets
And have received wide acclaim.

Yuan of Daozhou shows brilliance.
Though born late, he can hold elders' respect
    in awe.
After reading his "Ballad of Chongling",
His superb ability, I suddenly saw.

Next, on reading his poem "After Rebels

Retreated",
I feel Jie is really the pillar of the state.
He is another Jia Yi advising the king in tears.
Like Kuang Heng, to documented sources his
    memorials can relate.

The prefect of Daozhou worries about
    commoners.
From his poems, his boundless energy shows.
These two verses shine like the fall moon.
Like stars, every word glows.

His effective rule resembles that of Shu Yu
    of Tang
And reminds me of Da Ting's style of
    simplicity.
When can the sealed edict come down
And name him, for a high post, as an
    appointee?

II

By then, lawsuits and imprisonments forever
    cease,
Not just the end of warfare.
Sad over exactions on the people,
With light taxes, he steers towards a society,
    joyous and fair.

I now know about the will of a righteous man,
To bypass self-advancement and leave
    commoners' interest unharmed.
His high mindedness is a cool gale shaking
    South Mountain.
When pampered, he acts as if alarmed.

A bigger official seal in his hand gives
    discomfort.
Retiring as a recluse is his delight.
Like Changqing, I have long-term diabetes
And think of the palace, day and night.

With an acute lung disease and diabetes,
I live as a wanderer in Baidi City.
After calling to my son to get paper and brush,
I lean on a small table in the balcony.

I make a verse as I groan,
In pale ink, with brush strokes askew.
Moved by his poem on danger and hardship,
I hope mine will fall into receptive ears of
    those I knew.

八哀詩：贈司空王安思禮

I

司空出東夷，童稚刷勁翮。追隨燕薊兒，
穎銳物不隔。服事哥舒翰，意無流沙磧。
未甚拔行閒，犬戎大充斥。短小精悍姿，
屹然強冠敵。貫穿百萬眾，出入由咫尺。
馬鞍懸將首，甲外控鳴鏑。洗劍青海水，
刻銘天山石。

II

九曲非外番，其王轉深壁。飛兔不近駕，
鷙鳥資遠擊。曉達兵家流，飽聞春秋癖。
胸襟日沈靜，蕭蕭自有適。潼關初潰散，
萬乘猶辟易。偏裨無所施，元帥見手格。
太子入朔方，至尊狩梁益。胡馬纏伊洛，
中原氣甚逆。

III

肅宗登寶位，塞望勢敦迫。公時徒步至，
請罪將厚責。際會清河公，閒道傳玉冊。
天王拜跪畢，讜議果冰釋。翠華卷飛雪，
熊虎互阡陌。屯兵鳳凰山，帳殿涇渭闢。

185

金城賊咽喉，詔鎮雄所搤。禁暴靖無雙，
爽氣春浙瀝。

IV

巷有從公歌，野多青青麥。及夫哭廟後，
復頌太原役。恐懼祿位高，悵望王土窄。
不得見清時，嗚呼就窀穸。永繫五湖舟，
悲甚田橫客。千秋汾晉閒，事與雲水白。
昔觀文苑傳，豈述廉頗傳。嗟嗟鄧大夫，
士卒終倒戟。

Eight Sources of Grief: Lord Wang Sili, Posthumously Made Minister of Works

I

The Minister of Works came from Koguryeo.
In childhood, his robust pinions got preened
    right.
He followed the lads of Yan and Ji.
His faculty of learning is piercing and bright,

Working for Geshu Han,
About desert sands, he did not care.
He was not much recognized in the ranks
When Tibetan invaders were everywhere.

186

Short, strong and unyielding,
He subdued enemies firmly in his way.
Leading his troops through countless foes,
He got in and out, no matter how far away.

From his saddle hung a rebel general's head.
Beyond his panoply, he controlled ringing
    arrows.
He washed his sword with Kokonor's waters.
On a rock of Tianshan, his carved inscription
    shows.

II

Nine Bends was not a client state.
Into deeper cliffs, the Tibetan king went.
Short trips are not for a rare horse like Flying
    Rabbit.
On striking afar, birds of prey have inborn
    skill and intent.

He knows well the theories of military
    strategists.
To be devoted to the Spring and Autumn
    Annals is his firm position.
Neat and quiet, he found the right niche,
Being calm and peaceful in disposition.

After the first rout at Tong Pass,
The monarch fled in fright.
He could do nothing in a lower rank.
The field marshal was hard caught in the
 flight.

The crown prince left for Shuofang.
His Majesty took refuge at Liang and Yi.
The morale in the Central Plain was very low.
Nomad horses harassed Yi and Luo endlessly.

III

Suzong ascended to the precious throne.
The situation was pressing in the frontiers at
 that time.
His Honor walked up to him
And in wait for heavy penalty, confessed his
 crime.

Meanwhile, the Duke of Qinghe
Sent forth jade regalia for Xuanzong's
 abdication.
Once the King of Heaven received it with
 respect.
Outspoken counsels led to Wang's absolution.

Imperial banners flutter like flying snow.
Like bears and tigers, warriors spread along
    pathways.
Troops are stationed at Phoenix Hill.
By Jing and Wei, his constructed tent
    palace stays.

The throat of the rebels was at Jincheng
With which, by palace orders, he got to be at
    grips like a hero.
Peerless in quelling uprisings,
He restored peace like rainy spring, crisp and
    mellow.

IV

Many fields of wheat look green in the wilds.
His followers sang in the village alleyways.
After the rites with tears were over in the
    ancestral temple,
Of his assignments in Taiyuan, the king
    spoke in praise.

A high rank of office gave him fear.
At the sight of the shrinking domain, he was
    depressed.
Without seeing peaceful times return,
He died and in a grave went to rest.

He wished to moor his boat forever at the
  Five Lakes.
Compared with retainers of Tian Heng, in
  deeper grief his followers did address.
For countless years by Fen and Jin,
Like cloud and water, his legacy is spotless.

I read the biographies of men of letters in the
  past.
The achievement of Lian Po is not told,
  needless to say.
Too bad, Deng, a commander of fortitude and
  courage,
Got killed by his troops, an act of treason in
  play.

八哀詩： 故司徒李公光弼

I

司徒天寶末， 北收晉陽甲。 胡騎攻吾城，
愁寂意不愜。 人安若泰山， 薊北斷右脅。
朔方氣乃蘇， 黎首見帝業。 二宮泣西郊，
九廟起頹壓。 未散河陽卒， 思明偽臣妾。
復自碣石來， 火焚乾坤獵。 高視笑祿山，

公又大獻接。異王冊崇勳，小敵信所怯。
擁兵鎮河汴，千里初妥帖。

II

青蠅紛營營，風雨秋一葉。內省未入朝，
死淚終映睫。大屋去高棟，長城掃遺堞。
平生白羽扇，零落蛟龍匣。雅望與英姿，
惻愴槐里接。三軍晦光彩，烈士痛稠疊。
直筆在史臣，將來洗箱篋。吾思哭孤冢，
南紀阻歸楫。扶顛永蕭條，未濟失利涉。
疲苶竟何人，灑涕巴東峽。

Eight Sources of Grief: Li Guangbi, the Former Minister of Education

In the last year of Tianbo, the Minister of
    Education
Collected Jinyang's weapons in the north.
Nomad cavalries attacked the town,
With silent grief and discontent coming forth.

Steadfast as Mount Tai, this man hit Jibei
And got a flank of rebel troops cut through.
Our palace at Shuofang felt more relaxed,
With royal success in the commoners' view.

191

Two successive kings wept in the west
    outskirts.
From ruins, the nine ancestral temples rose.
The Heyang troops were not disbanded.
Shi Siming claimed his status as a subject
    in a pose.

Then Shi came down from Jie Rock,
Set fire to the universe to extirpate
And laughed at An Lushan with disdain.
His Honor's victory over Shi was great.

Not in the imperial line, the enfeoffed prince
    got high merits.
Bold before big foes, he heeded lesser ones
    with fear.
With his troops guarding the Yellow River
    and Bian Canal,
For endless miles, stability and peace could
    first appear.

II

Like blue flies, slanderers dominate the court.
Like a leaf in a fall rainstorm, goals are easily
    upset.
Awaken to his refusal to help the king,
Until death, he let his eyelashes soak in

tears of regret.

Without him, it was like a big house losing
  a high beam
Or a great wall with battlements that could
  not remain.
He was another Zhuge Liang with a white
  feathered fan,
Now a detained flood dragon on the wane.

Looking graceful and heroic,
In a grave near the tombs of kings, sadly he
  has lain.
It cast a gloom on the imperial army.
Brave soldiers suffered from heaps of pain.

Documents will be whitewashed in future.
The palace historian is to record honestly.
I want to weep before his lonely grave.
To set sail in the south for home I am not free.

I missed when it was right to venture.
Forever, help to the needy hardly appears.
Who really is this worn and weary man?
In the gorges, east of Ba, I am in tears.

示獠奴阿段

山木蒼蒼落日曛，竹竿裹裹細泉分。郡人
入夜爭餘瀝，豎子尋源獨不聞。病渴三更
迴白首，傳聲一注溼青雲。曾驚陶侃胡奴
異，怪爾常穿虎豹群。

For my Nomad Servant, A Duan

Hillside trees look dark green in sunset's light.
Slender bamboos softly sway; a tiny spring
    clearly comes in sight.
Look for water, only my servant has not been
    heard.
Fellow villagers fight for the last drop of
    water into the night.
One peel of thunder and blue clouds are wet.
With diabetes, I turn my white-haired head at
    midnight.
I was once awed by the uniqueness of Tao
    Kan's nomad servant.
You amaze me by often crossing areas with
    rebels on site.

園官送菜

序： 園官送菜把，本數日闕。矧苦苣，馬齒，掩乎嘉蔬，傷小人妒害君子，菜不足道也，比而作詩。

清晨蒙菜把，　常荷地主恩。　守者慚實數，
略有其名存。　苦苣刺如針，　馬齒葉亦繁。
青青嘉樹色，　埋沒在中園。　園吏未足怪，
世事因堪論。　嗚呼戰伐久，　荊棘暗長原。
乃知苦苣輩，　侵奪蕙草根。　小人塞道路，
為態何喧喧。　又如馬齒盛，　氣擁葵荏昏。
點染不易虞，　絲麻雜羅紈。　一經器物內，
永掛轆刺痕。　志士采紫芝，　放歌避戎軒。
畦丁負籠至，　感動百慮端。

A Gardener Sends me Vegetables

Preface: A gardener sends me a bunch of vegetables, but he has been lax for several days. Moreover, the bitter lettuce and horse-tooth amaranth overwhelm the better vegetables. I feel hurt that fine gentlemen are harmed by petty people. It is not worth discussing vegetables but the comparison makes me write a poem.

At dawn, favored with a bunch of greens,
I am always grateful of the landowner's grace.
The gardener is casual about the counts.
It is a mere gesture on the surface.

The bitter lettuce has thorn-like needles.
The lush leaves of the horse-tooth amaranth
    are also seen.
Buried in the central garden
Are fine vegetables looking so green.

It is not worth blaming the gardener.
On social events, our discussions should go.
O death! Wars are protracted.
On our long plains, thorns and brambles cast
    a shadow.

Now I realize things, like bitter lettuces,
Can get fragrant herbs uprooted and
    overthrown.
Petty people block the roads.
How loud and pushy are their manners shown!

Also the lush horse-tooth amaranths
Choke mallows and perillas with their energy.
It is not easy to guard against impurity.
From the mix with strands of hemp, fine
    silk is not free.

They leave permanent scars and scratches,
Once placed inside cookware.
Men of lofty principles pluck purple lingzhis.
They sing as hermits to avoid warfare.
When the gardener arrives with the baskets,
I get moved by the myriad sources of care.

船下夔州郭宿雨濕不得上岸別王十二判官

依沙宿舸船，石瀨月娟娟。風起春燈亂，
江鳴夜雨懸。晨鐘雲外濕，勝地石堂煙。
柔櫓輕鷗外，含悽覺汝賢。

Going Downstream by Boat to Kuizhou, I Spent the Night Outdoors, Got Wet and Could not Go Ashore to Part with Administrative Assistant Wang, the Twelfth

By sands, in the boat I stay overnight,
On rocky shallows falls charming moonlight.
The rising spring wind causes flickering
   lamplight.
A hanging sheet of rain rumbles on the river
   at night.

Dawn bells, moisture beyond clouds
And Stone Hall in mists create a scenic site.
Sadly I feel your sagacity,
On my soft-paddled boat, by gulls so light.

垂白

垂白馮唐老，清秋宋玉悲。江喧長少睡，
樓廻獨移時。多難身何補，無家病不辭。
甘從千日醉，未許七哀詩。

Hanging White Hair

With hanging white hair, Feng Tang was
    finally promoted by the king.
In clear fall, Song Yu was in grief.
The tall tower stands as time passes on.
By a noisy river, my sleep is brief.
During many calamities, what does my
    existence count?
To a wanderer's illness, there is no relief.
I am willing to drink for a hundred days.
Writing poems like "Seven Sources of
    Sorrow" is not what I can achieve,

幽人

孤雲亦群遊，神物有所歸。麟鳳在赤霄，
何當一來儀。往與惠荀輩，中年滄州期。
天高無消息，棄我忽若遺。內懼非道流，
幽人見瑕疵。洪濤隱語笑，鼓枻蓬萊池。
崔嵬扶桑日，照耀珊瑚枝。風帆倚翠蓋，
暮把東皇衣。嚶嗽元和津，所思煙霞微。
知名未足稱，局促商山芝。

Hermits

A lone cloud may also roam in company.
Deities return to their home grounds to stay.
Unicorn and phoenix are among red clouds.
When will they come forward in display?

In my mid-life, at the gray hermits' isles,
I hope to meet Huiyuan and Xu Xun of a
    former day.
With no news from them in the distant sky,
I feel abandoned and put away.

Recluses see my faults.
To be outside the mainstream of Daoism, I
    fear.
Great Billow, a Daoist hermit, hides his

speech and smile.
Towards the pool of Penglai, he moves his
  sweep to steer.

The towering sun rising from Fusang
Shines on coral twigs and makes them bright.
He leans on a green awning by sails in the
  wind,
Wearing the robe of the Lord King of the
  East at twilight.

He drinks and rinses from Primal Harmony
  Ford.
And yearns for faint cloud and mist.
Fame deserves no commendation.
Hidden and valued like Lingzi, hermits of
  Mount Shang exist.

白帝城最高樓

城尖徑昃旌旆愁，獨立縹緲之飛樓。峽坼
雲霾龍虎睡，江清日抱黿鼉遊。扶桑西枝
對斷石，弱水東影隨長流。杖藜嘆世者誰
子，泣血迸空回白頭。

The Highest Tower of White Emperor Fortress

The angular fortress with flags and paths
  aslant has a sad undertone.
By the soaring tower, far and dim, I stand
  alone.
Dragon and tiger sleep under clouds at the
  fissure of the gorge.
Swimming turtles and lizards in the sunlit,
  limpid river are shown.
West branches of the Fusang tree face broken
  rocks.
Setting light from the east on River Ruo has
  always flown.
I turn my head of white hai with blood and
  tears in a spray.
Who, on a cane, sighs for the state of the
  world as known?

秋行官張望督促東渚耗稻向畢清晨遣女奴
阿稽豎子阿段往問

東渚雨今足，佇聞粳稻香。上天無偏頗，
蒲稗各自長。人情見非類，田家戒其荒。
功夫競揰揰，除草置岸旁。穀者命之本，

201

勤懇免亂常。
豐苗亦已慨，
靜一資堤防。
茢揚用土暖，
用心未甚臧。
西成聚必散，
感此亂世忙。
荏苒百工休，

青春具所務，
並驅動莫當。
有生固蔓延，
提攜頗在綱。
尚恐主守疏，
寄語逾崇岡。
豈要仁里譽，
蟋蟀近中堂。

客居安可忘。
吳牛力容易，
雲水照方塘。
督領不無人，
蕭蕭候微霜。
清朝遣婢僕，
不獨陵我倉。
北風吹蒹葭，
鬱紆遲暮傷。

In Autumn, after Field Supervisor Zhang Wang has Finished Overseeing the Weeding of the Paddies at East Isle, at Dawn, I send my Maid A Ji and Servant A Duan there to Inquire

Now there is enough rain at East Isle.
I expect to hear about the fragrance of rice
    that people tell.
Heaven above has been fair.
Rushes and Weeds grow just as well.

People tend to watch for different things.
Farmers guard against land going to waste.
They leave pulled weeds by the shore,
After competing in digging in haste.

Grains are the essences of life.
As a sojourner, how can I forget?
Early spring fills the needs in our projects.
All work hard to avoid schedules being upset.

The strength of buffaloes comes easily.
In pairs, they move unopposed everywhere.
Paddies are packed with thriving sprouts.
Cloud and water shine in a pool like a square.

All things by nature want to propagate,
Especially one that deserves our heed.
A supervisor is not lacking.
Discipline in leadership is much in need.

In warm Jingzhou and Yangzhou,
The frost waited for quietly is light.
There is fear that the supervisor is careless
And the scheme in his mind is not right.

At dawn, I send words beyond high ridges,
From my servants, for the supervisor to know.
What is collected from the autumn harvest
Should not, in our granaries, just overflow.

Moved by the hustle of this world in turmoil,
I do not seek the fame of a humane neighbor
    at all.

The north wind will blow on reeds.
In deep winter, crickets are in the middle hall.

In time, all activities will wane.
Depression at the year's end causes me pain.

夔州歌十絕句，其一

中巴之東巴東山，江水開闢流其間。白帝
高為三峽鎮，夔州險過百牢關。

Kuizhou Songs: Ten Quatrains, no.1

East of Middle Ba is Badong County's hill.
White Emperor Fortress is a town of Three
　　Gorges way uphill.
After excavations, the river runs in between.
Compared with Bailao Pass, Kuizhou is more
　　dangerous still.

夔州歌十絕句，其二

白帝夔州各異城，蜀江楚峽混殊名。英雄
割據非天意，霸王并吞在物情。

Kuizhou Songs: Ten Quatrains, no.2

As cities, White Emperor Fortress and
  Kuizhou are not the same.
Shu rivers and Chu gorges are mixed in name.
It is not Heaven's will to have strong
  contending warlords.
On materialistic things, hegemonic kings
  want to lay claim.

夔州歌十絕句，其三

群雄競起問前期，王者無外見今朝。比訝
漁陽結怨恨，元聽舜日舊簫韶。

Kuizhou Songs: Ten Quatrains, no.3

Look to past dynasties for warlords who vied
  to stay.
A king with no foreign land has not fled
  today.
We were shocked by the hatred of rebels
  from Yuyang.
They followed the fine culture of Xuanzong,
  like that of King Shun of yesterday.

夔州歌十絕句，其四

赤甲白鹽俱刺天，閭閻繚繞接山巔。楓林
橘樹丹青合，榪道重樓錦繡懸。

Kuizhou Songs: Ten Quatrains, no.4

Both Red Shell and White Salt can pierce the
    sky.
All the way to the peak, winding hamlets lie.
Maple groves and orange trees create a
    painting.
As hanging brocade and embroidery, many
    paths and layered towers qualify.

夔州歌十絕句，其五

瀼東瀼西一萬家，江北江南春冬花。背飛
鶴子遺瓊蕊，相趁鳧雛入蔣牙。

Kuizhou Songs: Ten Quatrains, no.5

East and west of the river, myriad households
    stay.
North and south of the stream, blooms appear
    on any spring or winter day.

Young cranes fly apart, leaving feathers like
    jade flowers behind.
Wild ducklings follow one another into wild
    rice sprouts in the same way.

夔州歌十絕句，其六

東屯稻畦一百頃，北有澗水通青苗。晴浴
狎鷗分處處，雨隨神女下朝朝。

Kuizhou Songs: Ten Quatrains, no.6

East Camp has a hundred acres of paddies.
Into fields of green sprouts, streams from the
    north can drain.
Casual and carefree gulls bathe in the sun,
    here and there.
Each dawn, the goddess comes with rain.

夔州歌十絕句，其七

蜀麻吳鹽自古通，萬斛之舟行若風。長年
三老長歌裏，白晝攤錢高浪中。

207

Kuizhou Songs: Ten Quatrains, no.7

Shu jute trades well with Wu salt, from
  history we can say.
Like wind, big cargo ships sail away.
Senior punters sing for a long time.
Among high waves, traders gamble during
  the day.

夔州歌十絕句，其八

憶昔咸陽都市合，山水之圖張賣時。巫峽
曾經寶屏見，楚宮猶對碧峰疑。

Kuizhou Songs: Ten Quatrains, no.8

I recall in the market of Xianyang,
Where landscape paintings were sold,
I saw Wu Gorges on precious screens.
My doubt on the Chu palace facing green
  peaks will still hold.

夔州歌十絕句，其九

閬風玄圃與蓬壺，中有高唐天下無。借問
夔州壓何處，峽門江腹擁城隅。

Kuizhou Songs: Ten Quatrains, no.9

Langfeng, Xuanpu, Penglai and Fanghu are
    for immortals.
In between is Gaotang, prime and peerless.
At the gorges' mouth, the river pushes against
    the city corners
If you ask where Kuizhou can make the mark
    to impress.

夔州歌十絕句，其十

武侯祠堂不可忘，中有松柏參天長。干戈
滿地客愁破，雲日如火炎天涼。

Kuizhou Songs: Ten Quatrains, no.10

About the memorial hall of Zhuge Liang, I do
    not forget.
As tall as the sky, pine and cypress can get.
The trees offer coolness on torrid days.

As a wanderer at war, I am not sad or upset.

晚晴

反照斜初徹，浮雲薄未歸。江虹明遠飲，
峽雨落餘飛。鳬雁終高去，熊羆覺自肥。
秋分客尚在，竹露夕微微。

Late Clearing

The reflective, slanting rays are just over.
Thin clouds due to return are out of sight.
A distinct rainbow afar drinks from the river.
Dying rain on the gorges seems to be in flight.
I sense the bears are getting fat.
Finally, ducks and wild geese leave at a
    height.
A wanderer is still here by Autumn Equinox.
Dews on bamboos are ever so faint by night.

聽楊氏歌

佳人絕代歌，獨立發皓齒。滿堂慘不樂，
響下清虛裏。江城帶素月，況乃清夜起。

老夫悲暮年，壯士淚如水。玉杯久寂莫，
金管迷宮徵。勿云聽者疲，愚智心盡死。
古來傑出士，豈待一知己。吾聞昔秦青，
側傾天下耳。

Listening to Miss Yang's Singing

She stands alone with her gleaming teeth.
The fair lady's singing has no peers.
The whole audience is led to a sad mood
By the notes through the clear void that
    everyone hears.
Moreover, in the quiet night,
On the riverside town, a bright moon appears.
This old man grieves over his life at twilight.
Like water, from the able-bodied come tears.
Jade cups of wine are long forgotten.
Accompanists with golden pipes do not
    follow.
Do not say the listeners are weary.
The foolish and wise are spellbound by her
    rhythm and flow.
More than one bosom friend was needed
By distinguished men since the bygone years.
I heard of an ancient musician, Qin Qing.
Just to him, all earthlings lent their ears.

江月

江月光如水，　高樓思殺人。　天邊常作客，
老去一沾巾。　玉露團清影，　銀河沒半輪。
誰家挑錦字，　滅燭翠眉顰。

The Moon In-stream

The moon in-stream glows in the waters.
In a high tower, longings can kill me.
For long a stranger at the verge of the sky,
On my kerchief, in an instant, an old man's
　　tears are set free.
Jade-like dews encircle its clear image,
With half an orb hidden by the Milky Way.
Who is the lady doing embroidery for her
　　man in the army?
With the candles out, her knit, blackened
　　brows stay.

移居夔州郭

伏枕雲安縣，　遷居白帝城。　春知催柳別，
江與放船清。　農事聞人說，　山光見鳥情。
禹功饒斷石，　且就土微平。

Moving my Residence to the Outskirts of Kuizhou

I moved to White Emperor Fortress
From Yunan County where I lay on my
  pillow.
My boat set sail on a clear river.
In my hurry to leave in spring, I am reminded
  by the willow.
I hear the good cheer of people on farming.
Manners of birds are seen with the hills
  aglow.
The legacy of King Yu left many cut stones.
A slightly flattened route is what I follow.

秋日夔府詠懷奉寄鄭監李賓客一百韻

I

絕塞烏蠻北，孤城白帝邊。飄零仍百里，
消渴已三年。雄劍鳴開匣，群書滿繫船。
亂離心不展，衰謝日蕭然。筋力妻孥問，
菁華歲月遷。登臨多物色，陶冶賴詩篇。
峽束滄江起，巖排石樹圓。排雲霾楚氣，
朝海蹴吳天。煮井為鹽速，燒畬度地偏。
有時驚疊嶂，何處覓平川。鸑鷜雙雙舞，

213

獼猴壘壘懸。碧蘿長似帶，錦石小如錢。
春草何曾歇，寒花亦可憐。獵人吹戍火，
野店印山泉。喚起搔頭急，扶行幾屐穿。
兩京猶薄產，四海絕隨肩。幕府初交群，
郎官幸備員。瓜時猶旅寓，萍泛苦夤緣。
藥餌虛狼藉，秋風灑靜便。開襟驅瘴癘，
明目掃雲煙。

II

高宴諸侯禮，佳人上客前。哀箏傷老大，
華屋艷神仙。南內開元曲，常時弟子傳。
法歌變聲轉，滿座涕潺湲。弔影夔州僻，
回腸杜曲煎。即今龍廄水，莫帶犬戎膻。
耿賈扶王室，蕭曹拱禦筵。乘威滅蜂蠆，
戮力劾鷹鸇。舊物森猶在，凶徒惡未悛。
國須行戰役，人憶止戈鋋。奴僕何知禮，
恩榮錯與權。胡星一彗孛，黔首遂拘攣。
哀痛絲綸切，煩苛法令蠲。業成陳始王，
兆喜出於畋。宮禁經綸密，臺階翊戴全。
熊羆載呂望，鴻雁美周宣。側聽中興主，
長吟不世賢。音徽一柱數，道里下牢千。
鄭李光時論，文章並我先。陰何尚清省，
沈宋歘聯翩。

III

律比崑崙竹，　音知燥濕弦。　風流俱善價，
愜當久忘荃。　置驛常如此，　登龍蓋有焉。
雖云隔禮數，　不敢墜周旋。　高視收人表，
虛心味道玄。　馬來皆汗血，　鶴唳必青田。
羽翼商山起，　蓬萊漢閣連。　管甯紗帽淨，
江令錦袍鮮。　東郡時題詩，　南胡日扣舷。
遠遊淩絕境，　佳句染華箋。　每欲孤飛去，
徒為百慮牽。　生涯已寥落，　國步乃迍邅。
衾枕成蕪沒，　池塘作棄捐。　別離憂悁悁，
伏臘涕漣漣。　露菊班豐鎬，　秋蔬影澗瀍，
共誰輪昔事。　幾處有新阡，　富貴空回首。
喧爭懶著鞭。　兵戈塵漠漠，　江漢月娟娟。
局促看秋燕，　蕭疏聽晚蟬。　雕蟲蒙記憶，
烹鯉問沈綿。

IV

卜羨君平杖，　偷存子敬氈。　囊虛把釵釧，
米盡拆花鈿。　甘子陰涼葉，　茅齋八九椽。
陣圖沙北岸，　市暨瀼西巔。　羈絆心常折，
棲遲病即痊。　紫收岷嶺芋，　白種陸池蓮
色好梨勝頰，　穰多栗過拳。　敕廚唯一味，
求飽或三鱣。　兒去看魚笱，　人來坐馬韉。
縛柴門窄窄，　通竹溜消消。　塹抵公畦稜，

村依野廟堧。
借問頻朝謁，
自覺坐能堅。
紫鸞無近遠，
明公各勉旃。
懇諫留匡鼎，
會是正陶甄。

缺籬將棘拒，
何如穩晝眠。
霧雨銀章澀，
黃雀任翩翾。
聲華夾宸極，
諸儒引服虔。

倒石賴藤纏。
誰云行不逮，
馨香粉署妍。
困學違從眾，
早晚到星躔。
不過輸鯁直，

V

宵旰憂虞軫，
青簡為誰編。
由來具飛楫，
門求七祖禪。
安石名高晉，
查上似張騫。
風期終破浪，
傷春怯杜鵑。
本自依迦葉，
橘井尚高褰。
晚聞多妙教，
頭陀琬琰鐫。
勇猛為心極，
鏡象未離銓。

黎元疾苦駢。
行路難何有，
暫擬控鳴弦。
落帆追宿昔，
昭王客赴燕，
披拂雲寧在，
水怪莫飛涎。
淡交隨聚散，
何曾籍偓佺。
東走窮歸鶴，
卒踐塞前愆。
眾香深黯黮，
清嬴任體屛。

雲臺終日畫，
招尋興已專。
身許雙峰寺，
衣褐向真詮。
途中非阮籍，
淹留景不延。
他日辭神女，
澤國遶迴旋。
爐峰生轉沔，
南征盡跕鳶。
顧凱丹青列，
幾地蕭芊芊。
金篦空刮眼，

On an Autumn Day in Kuizhou, I Express my Thoughts in a Poem of a Hundred Couplets which is Sent Respectfully to Director Zheng and Li, Advisor to the Heir Apparent

I

At this remote north frontier with Wu nomads,
In a lonesome town, by White Emperor
    Fortress, I stay.
I have wandered for a hundred miles.
After three years, diabetes has not gone away.

A male sword in a shut chest rattles for
    freedom and action.
Books fill my boat everywhere,
I am ill at ease, in war and separation,
Quiet as I wane, from daily wear and tear.

My wife and children ask about my strength.
Essences of my life change as time goes by.
Climbing allows me to catch fine views.
To cultivate my spirit, on poems I rely.

Rows of trees stand before rocky cliffs.
In narrow gorges, waters of the gray river rise.
Fog and mist of Chu brush clouds.

Towards the sun, waves can kick at Wu skies.

Boil well water for a fast supply of salt.
To burn fields, choose one at a remote site,
Where can I find flat landscape?
At times, layered hilly barriers give me fright,

Wood ducks dance in pairs.
Monkeys hang in clusters, one and all.
Green creepers resemble long sashes.
Like coins, precious stone pebbles look small.

When does spring grass stop sprouting?
Flowers look lovely in the chill.
Hunters fan up their encampment fires.
A spring is led to a country inn from a hill.

When called up, I scratch my head feeling
    pushed.
With almost worn clogs, I walk with a cane.
In the two capitals, with meager assets,
I find no friends all over with me again.

When I first joined the headquarters,
To be on the temporary staff, I was fortunate.
Like ripe melons, my term matures with no
    permanency.
Like duckweeds adrift, I accept my bitter fate.

My scattered medicine offers no relief.
Puffs of fall wind lend quietude and ease.
I loosen my lapel to dispel miasma.
Without cloud and mist, vision will increase.

II

Grand feasts open with rites for high officials.
Fair ladies come to greet each guest.
Mournful zither tunes sadden this old man.
Like a fairy, the grand mansion looks its best.

The South Palace Troupe left melodies
That in the reign of Kaiyuan, had begun.
At the varied tones of dharma songs,
Tears stream down from everyone.

Homesickness sears up my twisting guts.
Alone in remote Kuizhou, I am in self-pity.
Now all the waters of the imperial stables,
From the stench of nomad troops, are not free.

Like Geng and Jin, our generals aid the king
And like Xiao and Cao, bow to the crown.
With might, they kill rebels like wasps and
    scorpions
And like birds of prey, bring them down.

Evil-mongers have not repented.
Old awe-inspiring law and order still remain.
The country should wage wars.
Commoners fondly recall any peaceful reign.

It was wrong to give rebels power and glory.
How can slaves know about being polite?
Once the nomads' star shines like a comet,
Commoners under control are bound tight.

Petty and harsh laws are now repealed.
The sad king wrote a decree from his heart.
Like a Zhou king, he seeks an able minister.
When all is done, his rule is to start.

Policies from the palace are in secret.
All lords give support to the court.
Like Lu Wang, our prime minister carries
    prestige and might.
On King Xuan of Zhou and our monarch,
    praise in history will be brought.

Let us listen to our leader of restoration
And chant in length on the peerless sage.
From One Pillar Lodge, Zheng often sends
    good new.
To reach Xialao Garrison, Li has endless

miles to engage.

As writers, Zheng and Li are ahead of me.
In their favor, current critics have opined.
Yin Keng and He Xun were admired for
    their clarity and brevity.
The sudden poetic flair of Shen Qianqi
    and Song Zhiwen was refined.

III

Your standard rhymes match those from
    Mount Kunlun's bamboo tubes.
Your tones are distinct and fine-tuned.
The poems you write are gallant and highly
    valued.
The medium is long forgotten once our
    hearts are attuned.

Zheng's name is often linked to lodges.
Li will rise in status, like passing the Dragon
    Gate.
Though my low status bars me from paying
    respects to you,
In my greetings, I dare not be slow or late.

Eyeing the exalted lends me a view of the
    praise-worthy.

A taste of the abstruse in Daoism comes from
    the vacuous mind.
Like horses that sweat blood, you are rare.
Like screeching, immortal cranes of Qingtian,
    you are of the same kind.

Like hermits of Mount Shang, Li helps the
    Heir Apparent.
Zheng heads the Imperial Library near the
    palace.
Like Guan Ning, Zheng is incorruptible.
The king's new brocade robe for Director
    Jiang is also for Li to embrace.

In East Command, Li at times inscribes on
    walls.
Zheng raps the boat's side on South Lake
    each day.
On long trips, they overlook top scenic spots.
Their letters are worded in a splendid way.

I always want to fly out alone to you,
But by countless worries, get held back.
My life is always dreary and bleak.
National progress is faltering with setback.

My quilt has gone to waste.
My pond is cast aside merely.

Parting gives me worries and grief.
On special days in summer or winter, I get
  very teary.

In Feng and Hao, dewy chrysanthemums
  thrive.
In Jian and Chan, shadows of fall vegetables
  are cast.
In how many places have paths been made?
With whom can I discuss the past?

My efforts for gain and power are in vain.
For such battles, I do not care to fight.
The dust of war spreads far and wide.
Above Yangzi and Han is pretty moonlight.

Ill at ease, I watch autumn swallows
And listen to night cicadas alone.
I am flattered by your memory of my humble
  writing
And, in your letters, the concern about my
  health shown.

IV

I envy Junping's life as a contented fortune-
  teller.
Save for heirlooms, I would give all to a thief.

223

With an empty purse, I fiddle with packets of
    hairpins.
With rice gone, I tear off floral filigrees for
    relief.

Orange leaves give shade and coolness.
On my thatched study, eight or nine beams
    rest.
North of the sandy banks lies the Eight-Part
    Battle Formation.
The city wharf is by the ridge of River West.

A detained wanderer is often heart-broken.
My illness has relief, in my long stay here.
Min Bridge has taros in purple.
In Lu Pool, white lilies appear.

Good pears may look better than cheeks.
Chestnuts full of flesh are bigger than fists,
    more or less.
The imperial order for the kitchen is only on
    one dish.
I need three sturgeons to fill my stomach for
    success.

Astride a saddle cover, a man comes on a
    horse.
To see the fish weir, my son goes.

My door is too narrow for bound firewood.
In bamboo pipes, water smoothly flows.

A ditch runs as far as the corner of a public
    plot.
In an empty lot, by a nameless temple, a
    village lies.
I use briars to block the gap of my hedge.
On the mesh of rattans, success of catching
    falling rocks relies.

Let me ask how frequent dawn courts are,
Compared with sound sleeps in daylight.
Who says I cannot sustain a walk?
I just feel I can sit and show fight.

In fog and rain, my silver badge of office
    shines no more.
The Secretariat looks imposing with its
    fragrance.
Like yellow birds, unknowns flit wherever
    they please.
Like purple phoenixes, high officials roam
    regardless of distance.

With little schooling, I do not write to please
    the crowds.
Roused to action, you wise gentlemen are

well-known.
You will be among the top, sooner or later,
With your fame and flair, assisting the throne.

Kuang Heng was retained for his earnest
  admonitions.
By various Confucian scholars, Fu Qian was
  well received.
If they are just being honest and direct,
Timing is right to adjust the wheel of
  governance, as conceived.

V

The king works hard, deeply worried.
The suffering of commoners is dire.
Portraits of war heroes are painted in the
  Cloud Palace all day.
For whom are compiled the history of the
  empire.

How hard is it to travel?
To seek scenic spots is my interest and intent.
All along, I am equipped with fast oars.
To control my fast boat is my plan at present.

As a disciple of Chan Buddhism, I shall seek
  the Seventh Patriarch.

At a temple of Twin Peaks, my faith is fast.
Dressed humbly, I shall head towards truth,
Lowering my sail to atone for my past.

Like King Zhao of Yan, Li is a descendant
of the Zhou house.
Like Anshi of Jin, Zhang earns great fame.
I resemble Zhang Qian on a raft exploring.
Ruan Ji wept when astray, but I am not the
same.

Like clouds brushed aside, I am nobody,
Just a detained wanderer, with a limited life
span.
When wind comes, I shall at last break waves.
Let water monsters stop drooling on this man.

In spring lament and fear of the cuckoo's call,
From the goddesses of Mount Wu, one day I
shall part.
I shall make my rounds in my voyage.
In casual friendship, it matters little being
together or apart.

Basically, I follow Kashyapa's teachings.
To depend on Woquan, the immortal, when
did I try?
Tangerines and wells of Fairyland are too

high to reach.
The peak of Mount Lu rose in the blink of
    an eye.

A crane put a harassed man on its back and
    flew east.
A general saw all kites drop in a miasmal,
    southern sky.
Of late, I came across the preaching of many
    subtleties in Buddhism.
Now any chance of repeating former mistakes,
    I finally deny.

The paintings of Gu Kaizhi are in display.
Dhuta Temple has a shiny jade stele
    inscription of Buddhist parallel prose.
Many fragrances run deep in the dark.
In several solemn spots, lush green grass
    grows.

I fought hard to reach the mind's ultimate
    state.
Pure and weak, I let my form be frail.
I have not detached myself from the virtual
    images in the mirror.
A gold comb shaving my eyeball for better
    vision will fail.

秋日寄題鄭監湖上亭三首， 其一

碧草違春意， 沅湘萬里秋。池要山簡馬，
月淨庾公樓， 磨滅餘篇翰， 平生一釣舟。
高唐寒浪減， 仿佛識昭丘。

On an Autumn Day, an Inscription Sent to Director Zheng on his Lakeside Pavilion in Three Poems, no.1

For endless miles, in fall at Yuan and Xiang,
Without vernal signs, green grass goes to
   blight.
Your lake can attract Shan Jian, the drinker,
   on horseback.
Your pavilion is another Yu Tower for
   watching clear moonlight.
I shall wane in time, leaving my writings.
For my life, a fishing boat is right.
At Gaotang, cold waves weaken.
King Zhao's mound is vaguely in sight.

秋日寄題鄭監湖上亭三首， 其二

新作湖邊宅，遠聞賓客過。自須開竹徑，
誰道避雲蘿。官序潘生拙，才名賈傅多。
含舟應卜地，鄰接意如何。

On an Autumn Day, an Inscription Sent to Director Zheng on his Lakeside Pavilion in Three Poems, no. 2

From afar, I heard of guests passing by
Your lakeside building constructed anew.
Who says you are hiding behind dense vines?
You should make a path by clumps of
    bamboo.
Like Pan Yue, you can claim ineptitude in
    rank and office.
Compared with Jia Yi, your talent and fame
    reach a greater height.
How would you like me as a neighbor?
After mooring, I should choose a site.

秋日寄題鄭監湖上亭三首，其三

暫阻蓬萊閣，終為江海人。揮金應物理，
拖玉豈吾身。烹煮秋蓴滑，杯迎露菊新。
賦詩分氣象，佳句莫頻頻。

On an Autumn Day, an Inscription Sent to Director Zheng on his Lakeside Pavilion in Three Poems, no.3

For now you are away from Penglai Pavilion,
To be finally at leisure by river and sea.
You spend your money according to your
    means and reason.
A court official with jade is not what we want
    to be.
With a stew of smooth water-shields in fall,
You have cups of wine with chrysanthemums,
    fresh and dewy.
Making poems on the energy and forms here,
We cannot help but let frequent fine lines run
    free.

題柏學士茅屋

碧山學士焚銀魚，白馬卻走身巖居。古人
已用三冬足，年少今開萬卷餘。晴雲滿戶
團傾蓋，秋水浮階溜決渠。富貴必從勤苦
得，男兒須讀五車書。

On the Thatched Cottage of Academician Bo

From his silver fish badge of office, the
    academician wants to go away.
Without his white horse, by a green cliff, he
    is to stay.
Spending three winters in a study was enough
    for ancients.
Endless books are opened by the young today.
Fall waters flood steps and drain via ditches.
Clustered clouds fully cover his door on a
    sunlit day.
A man needs to read five cartloads of books.
Fame and gain must be what hard work will
    pay.

奉贈蕭十二使君

I

昔在嚴公幕，　俱為蜀使臣。　艱危參大府，
前後問清塵。　起草鳴先路，　乘槎動要津。
王鳧聊暫出，　蕭雉只相馴。　終始任安義，
荒蕪孟母鄰。　聯翩匍匐禮，　意氣死生親。
張老存家事，　嵇康有故人。　食恩慚鹵莽，
鏤骨抱酸辛。　巢許山林志，　夔龍廊廟珍。
鵬圖仍矯翼，　雄軾且移輪。

II

磊落衣冠地，　蒼茫土木身。　塤箎鳴自合，
金石瑩逾新。　重憶羅江外，　同遊錦水濱。
結歡隨過隙，　懷日益沾巾。　曠絕含香舌，
稽留伏枕辰。　停驂雙闕早，　回雁五湖春。
不達長卿病，　從來原憲貧。　監河受貸粟，
一起轍中鱗。

Respectfully Presented to Governor Xiao, the Twelfth

Both as Lord Yan's subordinates in Shu,
We worked in his headquarters years ago.

233

In peril, we labored to manage the place.
First you missed his moral leadership
   and I now follow.

Early on, recognized as a writer of drafts,
As if on a fairy's raft you could go.
Briefly you served as a county judge.
Like Xiao Zhiwei, you are the director of a
   bureau.

You care about Yan's mother.
Like Ren An, righteousness is your motto.
You crawl to pay respects in Yan's funeral.
In life and death, friendliness you show.

Like Old Zhang, you are concerned about his
   family.
An old friend raised Ji Kang's son; you will
   take Yan's son in also.
Unable to repay Yan, I am ashamed by my
   rashness.
With guilt etched in my bones, I am in deep
   sorrow.

Like Ge Chaofu and Xu You, I like hill and
   forest.
Like Kui and Long, in the palace Hall of
   Fame, your esteem will grow.

I still plan to use the strong wings of a roc.
In your exalted post, you will use a bear on
  your carriage as a logo.

II

You are open to the public, among caps and
  gowns.
I am obscure and lost, stuck in soil and wood
  below.
Like Xun and Chi, we sound off in the same
  tempo.
Like metal and stone, we offer fresher notes
  in duo.

We toured Luoyang and by Brocade River.
These scenes in my memory can echo.
Our joyous outings passed quickly.
My kerchief gets more tears of homesickness
  and woe.

I cannot have an audience with the king.
Well detained here, I spend time lying on my
  pillow.
At the double palace gates, you stop your
  carriage early.
Like a homebound wild goose in spring,
  retiring in the Five Lakes is my credo.

Like Changqing, I am sick and a failure.
Like Yuan Xian, I am always poor as you
    know.
In the same plight as a fish caught on a wheel
    rut,
From the Count of Jianhe, I trust there should
    be grains to borrow.

送田四弟將軍將夔州柏中丞命起居江陵節度陽城郡王衛公幕

離筵罷多酒，起地發寒塘。回首中丞座，
馳箋異姓王。燕辭楓樹日，雁度麥城霜。
空醉山翁酒，遙憐似葛疆。

Seeing off General Tian, the Fourth, Following the Orders of Vice-Censor Bo of Kuizhou, to Pay his Respects at the Headquarters of Lord Wei, Prince of Yangcheng Commandery and Military Commissioner of Jiangling

He will set out from a cold pool,
After a parting feast with much wine.
Turning his head towards the vice-censor's

seat,
He will bring a letter to a prince off the
imperial family line.
Wild geese cross the frost of Mai Cheng.
Swallows fly off maple groves and the sun.
In vain, he will be as drunk as Shan Jian,
But like Ge Qiang, treated as the favorite
general, next to none.

送顧八分文學適洪吉州

I

中郎石經後，八分蓋憔悴。顧侯運爐錘，
筆力破餘地。昔在開元中，韓蔡同贔屭。
玄宗妙其書，是以數子至。禦扎早流傳，
揄揚非造次。三人並入直，恩澤各不二。
顧於韓蔡內，辨眼工小字。分日示諸王，
鉤深法更祕。文學與我游，蕭疏外聲利。
追隨二十載，浩蕩長安醉。高歌卿相宅，
文翰飛省寺。視我揚馬間，白首不相棄。
驊騮入窮巷，必脫黃金彎。一論朋友難，
遲暮敢失墜。

II

古來事反覆，　相見橫涕泗。　嚮者玉珂人，
誰是青雲器。　才盡傷形體，　病渴汙官位。
故舊獨依然，　時危話顛躓。　我甘多病老，
子負憂世志。　胡為困衣食，　顏色少稱遂。
遠作苦辛行，　順從眾多意。　舟楫無根蒂，
蛟鼉好為崇。　況兼水賊繁，　特戒風飆駛。
崩騰戎馬際，　往往殺長吏。　子干束諸侯，
勸勉防縱恣。　邦以民為本，　魚饑費香餌。
請哀瘝痍深，　告訴皇華使。　使臣精所擇，
進德知歷試。　惻隱誅求情，　固應賢愚異。
列士惡苟得，　俊傑思自致。　贈子猛虎行，
出郊載酸鼻。

Seeing off Instructor Gu, Master of the Bafen Script of Calligraphy, for Hongzhou and Jizhou

I

After the carved classics on stone by a court
　gentleman,
The disfavored Bafen Script was found.
Lord Gu forged his strokes in calligraphy,
With a force that broke new ground.

In the Kaiyuan reign in the past,
Forceful brush writing of Han Zemu and Cai
   Youlin was shown.
Xuanzong marveled at their work
And admitted both before the throne.

Royal announcements circulated early.
Commendations were random from the
   palace.
These three men went to the court together,
Each receiving the same favor and grace.

Gu, in the same class as Han and Cai,
Specialized in small, fine characters, with
   his discerning eyes.
The art was shared with the princes for days.
Bold outlines and mythical rules were for
   them to recognize.

The instructor went about with me,
Free and easy, without concern for fame or
   gain.
We followed each other for twenty years,
Drunk in Changan, letting go again and again.

We chanted loudly in high officials' homes.
Our writings flew into government offices in
   a pair.

He thought of me equal to Yang Xiong and
    Sima Xiangru
And would not abandon me with white hair.

When a rare horse enters rundown lanes,
Its gold bridle must be tossed.
People say it is hard to keep friends,
In my decline, dare I let friendships be lost.

II

Things always change since ancient times.
As we meet, our tears run free.
Of those in important offices in the past,
To reach the very top, who could that be?

My talent is gone and my body weakened.
Sick in diabetes, I leave any official position
    a stain.
In perilous times, I talk about life's stumbles
    and falls.
Unchanged, only my old associates remain.

You care about the world and want to help.
I accept being old and in disease.
Why is it you are still hard up in livelihood?
Your look tells me few things go as you
    please.

You travel in hardship afar.
The majority will followed is predominant.
A boat has no roots to anchor.
Flood dragons and crocodiles like to be
  dominant.

What is more, pirates proliferate.
Under strong winds, sail with special care.
Our senior officials are usually killed
As we stumble and dodge during warfare.

You will seek an audience with the lords
  of the east.
Tell them people form the base of the state.
Advise them against indulgence.
Feed hungry fish with a fragrant bait.

Please feel the commoners' deep ulcers.
Relay to palace envoys complaints attested.
Officials for liaison were carefully chosen,
With better morals and much tested.

Sympathize with those pleading their cases.
Sages and fools should be different.
Should ordinary people do wrong by chance.
The best and brightest should not be egoistic
  and indifferent.

Let me present you the "Ballad of the Fierce
  Tiger" on honesty.
You will feel like crying as you leave the city.

官亭夕坐戲簡顏十少府

南國調寒杵，西江浸日車。客愁連蟋蟀，
亭古帶蒹葭。不返青絲鞚，虛燒夜燭花。
老翁須地主，細細酌流霞。

Sitting in the Official Pavilion in the Evening, I Send a Playful Note to Sheriff Yan, the Tenth

In the south, mallets are beaten in the cold.
West River gets soaked in sunshine.
Crickets make a wanderer feel sad.
By an old pavilion, reeds and rushes grow in
  line.
Not returning with your blue silk halter,
In vain, at night you let her candles shine.
This old man needs a host
To pour me fine streams of the fairies' wine.

阻雨不得歸瀼西柑林

三伏適已過，驕陽化為霖。欲歸瀼西宅，
阻此江浦深。壞舟石板坼，峻岸復萬尋。
篙工初一棄，恐泥勞寸心。佇立東城隅，
悵望高飛禽。常堂亂懸圖，不隔昆侖岑。
昏渾衣裳外，曠絕同層陰。園柑長成時，
三寸如黃金。諸侯舊上計，厥貢傾千林。
邦人不足重，所迫蒙吏侵。客居暫封植，
日夜偶瑤琴。虛徐五株態，側寒煩胸襟。
焉得輟雨足，杖藜出嶇嶔。條流數翠實，
偃息歸碧潯。拂拭烏皮几，喜聞樵牧音。
令兒快搔背，脫我頭上簪。

Stranded by Rain, I am Unable to Return To the Orange Groves of River West

Just after the third day from Summer Solstice,
The torrid sun is replaced by heavy rain.
I wanted to return to my home by River West,
But got well stranded without an inch to gain.

The worn boat has a hundred broken planks.
Steep banks are countless yards high.
Boatmen at once give up on handling mud,
In fear of a hearty but fruitless war if they try.

I stand in wait at the corner of East Town,
Depressed by high flying birds in sight.
My humble hut mars the landscape, like
    Hanging Garden of Fairyland,
But blocks no ridge like Mount Kunlun with
    its height.

Everything beyond my robe is a gloomy mess,
In the widest space, with darkness in the
    same mold.
When oranges in orchards are fully grown,
They are three inches thick, yellow like gold.

Some past, local dignitaries offered a plan,
Using oranges from endless groves as tributes.
Unvalued commoners of this domain
Got taken by officials like brutes

As a stranger here, I planted these trees
Which at times rustle like zithers, each night
    and day.
The five trees look calm and relaxed.
I feel vexed for being stranded on my way.

How can I stop the rain
And leave the rugged, tall hill on my cane?
I shall count the jade-like fruits on twigs
Before resting by a blue stream again.

Songs of woodcutters and herders cheer me.
I wipe and clean my leather tray in black.
With hairpins off my head,
I shall ask my son to scratch my back.

客堂

I

憶昨離少城，　而今異楚蜀。　捨舟復深山，
窈跳一林麓。　棲泊雲安縣，　消中內相毒。
舊疾廿載來，　衰年得無足。　死為殊方鬼，
頭白免短促。　老馬終望雲，　南雁意在北。
別家長兒女，　欲起慚筋力。　客堂序節改，
具物對羈束。　石暄紫蕨芽，　渚秀蘆筍綠。
巴鶯紛未稀，　微麥早向熟。

II

悠悠日動江，　漠漠春辭木。　臺郎選才俊，
自顧亦已極。　前輩聲名人，　埋沒何所得。
居然絟章綬，　受性本幽獨。　平生憩息地，
必種數竿竹。　事業只濁醪，　營葺但草屋。
上公有記者，　累奏資薄祿。　主憂豈濟時，

245

身遠彌曠職。循文廟算正，獻可天衢直。
尚想趨朝廷，毫髮裨社稷。形骸今若是，
進退委行色。

A Wanderer's Hall

I

I recall leaving West Chengdu, the minor city.
To Kuizhou of former Chu, I now come.
I left my boat for the deep mountains
For the wooded foothills, far and winsome.

I moored and lodged in Yunan County.
My diabetes is poisoning me inside,
An age-old disease for twenty years.
As I wane, have I not had enough alongside?

I shall die as a ghost on a strange land,
White-haired with a short life henceforth.
I am a tired old horse, gazing at clouds
And a southbound wild goose with ambitions
    in the north.

My frailty shames me as I try to rise.
Since leaving home, my children have grown.
In a wanderer's hall, with seasonal and other

changes,
To lose control over things, I am prone.

Purple fern leaves sprout by sunlit rocks.
On a pretty isle, green asparagus appears.
Orioles in Ba gather in groups still.
Wheat ripens early in the frontiers.

II

The sun keeps bringing life to the river.
Spring is leaving trees quietly.
The talented are chosen from recruitment
    platforms.
I can find excellence in me.

Famed people of an earlier generation
Got neither gain nor chances to be of use.
Unexpectedly I got a badge of offer.
I am by nature a loner and a recluse.

In my life, wherever I live,
I must plant some strands of bamboo.
My job is only dealing with unfiltered wine.
Repairing just a thatched cottage is what I do.

A high official has me in mind.
After repeated petitions, I got a meager pay.

How can I aid the worried king and the times?
From the court, I am too lapsed and far away.

An enlightened court follows the right course.
Petitions to the court should be easy and
    straight.
I imagine myself hurrying for the palace,
In a small way to help the state.
With my body as it is now,
My going forward or backward depends on
    all conditions to date.

小至

天時人事日相催，冬至陽生春又來。刺繡
五紋添弱線，吹葭六管動飛灰。岸容待臘
將舒柳，山意衝寒欲放梅。雲物不殊鄉國
異，教兒且覆掌上杯。

Winter Solstice Eve

Seasons and human affairs hurry us each day.
Winter Solstice tells the sun and vernal
    effects are again coming.
Another thread is added to the embroidery
    with five stripes.

Reed ashes flying up in six pipes when blown
  signal a dormant spring.
Awaiting for the new year, willows at the
  shore will sprout.
Of the cold hill, blossoming plums think
  nothing.
I tell my son to pour more wine into my cup
  in hand.
In this strange land, there is similarity in
  nature and everything.

行官張望補稻畦水歸

東屯大江北， 百傾平若案。 六月青稻多，
千畦碧泉亂。 插秧適云已， 引溜加溉灌。
更僕往方塘， 決渠當斷案。 公私各地著，
浸潤無天旱。 主守問家臣， 分明見溪畔。
芊芊炯翠羽， 剡剡生銀漢。 鷗鳥鏡裏來，
關山雲邊看， 秋菰成黑米， 精鑿傳白粲。
玉粒足晨炊， 紅鮮任霞散。 終然添旅食，
作苦期壯觀。 遺穗及眾多， 我倉戒滋蔓。

Zhang Wang, Field Supervisor, Returns after Improving the Irrigation of Paddy Fields

North of the big river, at East Camp,
Like a table, huge flat acres show the land's
lay.
In the sixth month, many paddy fields look
green.
Emerald-like streams on countless lots run in
disarray.

Conduits are made to improve irrigation,
Right after the planting of rice sprouts is done.
Workers in shifts set out for the square pond,
From which through ditches with sharp banks,
water can run.

With soaked fields, there is no drought,
For private and public plots, at every site.
As the chief of the project, I ask my staff
for feedback.
Paddy fields look like creeks with banks,
clear and bright.

The lush growth emits a glow, like
the kingfisher's feather.
Sharp tips in fields create the Milky Way.

Gulls come with their reflections on water
like a mirror.
Watch the edge of clouds where passes and
hills stay.

In fall, black wild rice matures.
Fine hulling produces seeds, white and shiny.
Jade-like rice makes substantial breakfasts.
Fresh red grains resemble clouds spread free.

In the end, they add to the diet of a wanderer.
A grand view is expected after toil and pain.
Leftovers will be shared with the public.
From using my granary as a miser's hoard,
I abstain.

Year 768-770

衡州送李大夫七丈勉赴廣州

斧鉞下青冥，樓船過洞庭。北風隨爽氣，
南斗避文星。日月籠中鳥，乾坤水上萍。
王孫丈人行，垂老見飄零。

At Hengzhou Seeing off Li Mian, Grand Master, on his Way to Guangzhou

From the court, to lead an army south you go.
Your warship crosses Lake Dongting's flow.
Southern rebels dodge from a literary man.
North winds make freshness follow.
I am a caged bird each day and night
And a duckweed afloat in this world I know.
Your trip is one for a princely, senior official.
Mine is taken by a wanderer and aging fellow.

潭州送韋員外牧韶州（迢）

炎海韶州牧，風流漢署郎。分符先令望，
同舍有輝光。白首多年疾，秋天昨夜涼。
洞庭無過雁，書疏莫相忘。

At Tanzhou, Seeing off Supernumerary Wei Tiao to his Post as Governor of Shaozhou

You will govern Shaozhou near the torrid sea,
A gallant official of our reign, in your right.
The seal of office, your first recognition,
Lets your colleagues share your limelight.
White-haired and in long-term illness,
I felt the autumn chill last night.
Let our friend endure with few letters.
Wild geese at Lake Dongting are out of
sight.

詠懷二首，其一

人生貴是男，丈夫重天機。未達善一身，
得志行所為。嗟予竟轗軻，將老逢艱危。
胡雛逼神器，逆節同所歸。河雒化爲血，
公侯草問啼。西京復陷沒，翠蓋蒙塵飛。

萬姓悲赤子，　兩宮棄紫微。　倏忽向二紀，
奸雄多是非。　本朝再樹立，　未及貞觀時。
日給在軍儲，　上官督有司。　高賢迫形勢，
豈暇相扶持。　疲苶苟懷策，　棲屑無所施。
先王實罪己，　愁痛正為茲。　歲月不我與，
蹉跎病於斯。　夜看鄮城氣，　回首蛟龍池。
齒髮已自料，　意深陳苦詞。

Chanting What is on My Mind, no.1

The male sex is valued in life.
Men take nature's rules to heart.
Accomplished, he practices what is right.
Before success, he grooms himself as a start.

Alas, I am down in luck,
In hardship and danger while getting old.
The nomad chick encroached upon our
　　divine empire,
With other rebels screaming in the same mold.

River Luo turned into a stream of blood.
Among grasses, noblemen wailed.
In defeat, the royalty fled in carriages,
After efforts to hold the west capital failed.

The whole royal family gave up the palaces.

Like children, commoners are in sorrow.
Rogue heroes have brought much contention.
Towards the second dozen years, fast we go.

The current government got re-established,
Out-matched by the Zhengguan reign.
Daily provisions are for the army,
A rule for the department head to retain.

Lofty sages are pushed by the circumstances.
How can they find time for mutual aid?
Worn and weary, should one hold a plan,
In a tough life, no action can be made.

The former king actually blamed himself,
Causing my sorrow and pain to appear.
Time slips by, against my will.
I wasted time being sick here.

By night, I watch the energy at Feng city,
In the flood dragon's pool, as I turn my head.
I can assess my health by my teeth and hair.
With deep emotion, let my bitterness be read.

詠懷二首，其二

邦危壞法則，聖遠益愁慕。飄飄桂水遊，
悵望蒼梧暮。潛魚不銜鉤，走鹿無反顧。
暚暚幽曠心，拳拳異平素。衣食相拘閡，
朋知限流寓。風濤上春沙，千里浸江樹。
逆行少吉日，時節空復度。井竈任塵埃，
舟航煩數具。牽纏加老病，瑣細隘俗務。
萬古一死生，胡為足名數。多憂汙桃源，
拙計泥銅柱。為辭炎瘴毒，擺落跋涉懼。
虎狼窺中原，焉得所歷住。葛洪及許靖，
避世常此路。賢愚誠等差，自愛各馳騖。
羸瘠且如何，魄奪針灸屢。擁滯僮僕慵，
稽留篙師怒。終當掛帆席，天意難告訴。
南為祝融客，勉強親杖屨。結托老人星，
羅浮展衰步。

Chanting What is on My Mind, no.2

The tottering state, lax on law enforcement,
Makes me long for a sage king and feel upset.
Depressed, I drift on the waters of Gui
And watch Mount Cangwu at sunset.

A bottom fish does not bite the hook.
A departing deer does not look back.
My heart for quiet, open spots is evident.

In special earnestness, I am not slack.

My friends are few due to my wanderings.
Food and clothing are hard to obtain.
Wind-swept billows climb sand bars in spring.
Riverside trees stand in a long flooded terrain.

I have little luck going upstream
And miss festivals again and again.
I am vexed often by problems on the voyage.
In dust, my well and stove are to remain.

Besides being old and sick,
I am hampered by tasks, petty and mundane.
For one's life until death, in the millennia,
In wealth and rank, what good comes from
    the gain?

Many worries mar the Peach Flower Stream.
The prestige of a bronze pillar gets soiled by
    poor planning at hand.
I do not retreat from heat and miasma,
Defying the fear of moving on water and land.

Like tiger and wolf, rebels peep at the
    Central Plain.
How can I settle down as I move on my way?
Ge Hong and Xu Jing

Were recluses often on this walkway.

Though wise men and fools differ in class,
For self-interest, pushy schemes are in play.
What is there for a frail person like me?
Acupuncture and moxibustion often take my
    soul away.

My servant gets inert if stuck in one place.
With the boatman's temper, a long stay does
    not go well.
Finally it is time to set sail.
Heaven's will is hard to tell.

I will visit Zhurong Peak in the south
And strive to be close to an alchemist and old
    fellow.
Let me befriend and entrust myself to the
    Old Man Star.
To Mount Luofu, my failing feet will go.

留別公安太易沙門

隱居欲就廬山遠，麗藻初逢休上人。數問
舟航留制作，長開篋笥擬心神。沙村白雪

仍含凍，江縣紅梅已逢春。先蹋爐峰置蘭
若，徐飛錫杖出風塵。

Detained on Parting by Monk Taiyi at Gongan

Being close to Monk Huiyuan of Mount Lu is my wish as a recluse..

To your fine writing like that of Monk Huixiu, I first have access.

You left your compositions as a frequent visitor to my boat.

Always from open baskets, your mind I can assess.

Pink plum flowers have opened in spring in this riverside county.

On the sands of this village, there is still unthawed snow.

You will first tread Censer Peak and present orchid an iris.

A relaxed flight with a tin staff, beyond wind and dust, will follow.

遣遇

磬折辭主人，開帆駕洪濤。春水滿南國，
朱崖雲日高。舟子廢寢食，飄風爭所操。
我行匪利涉，謝爾從者勞。石間采蕨女，
鬻菜輸官曹。丈夫死百役，暮返空村號。
聞見事略同，刻剝及錐刀。貴人豈不仁，
視汝如莠蒿。索錢多門戶，喪亂紛嗷嗷。
奈何黠吏徒，漁奪成逋逃。自喜遂生理，
花時甘縕袍。

Expressing my Experiences

I took leave of my host after bowing humbly
And set sail on waves with might.
In spring, Southland is fully flooded.
Above red cliffs, sunlit clouds are at a height.
Boatmen forego sleep and food.
With whirling winds, they want to fight.
Thank you, the crew, for your labor.
On my trip, for material gains I have no
　　appetite.
A woman picking vetches among rocks sell
　　them for cash,
which goes to officials who get their right.
Her husband died after endless toil.
She returns to an empty village, crying at

twilight.
Villagers are chiseled and knifed cruelly.
From what I have seen or heard, all are in
the same plight.
How can those in high ranks be so inhumane?
Commoners are just foxtails and mugworts,
in their sight.
Excuses for demanding cash are many.
With death and unrest, wailing is heard from
site to site.
Nothing can be done to crafty, evil officials
Who after exploitations, flee from justice as
if in flight.
I am happy with my conduct of life.
In a hempen robe, in a season with flowers,
I feel alright.

夜聞觱篥

夜聞觱篥滄江上，衰年側耳情所嚮。鄰舟
一聽多感傷，寒曲三更欻悲壯。積雪飛霜
此夜寒，孤燈急管復風湍。君知天下干戈
滿，不見江湖行路難。

Hearing the Bili at night

I heard the bili on a gray river at night.
Drawn to the music, in my waning years, I
   listened tight.
The notes from the next boat put me in a sad
   plight.
Tragically heroic, the mood caught me at
   once in the chill of midnight.
With drifting snow and flying frost, it is cold
   tonight.
As winds churn, fast tunes float by a lone
   lamp's light.
Sir, you may know about the whole world
   engaged in fight,
But the hardship of traveling on land and
   water is out of sight.

舟中出江陵南浦奉寄鄭少尹（審）

更欲投何處，　飄然去此都。　形骸元土木，
舟楫復江湖。　社稷纏妖氣，　干戈送老儒。
百年同棄物，　萬國盡窮途。　雨洗平沙淨，
天銜闊岸紆。　鳴螿隨汎梗，　別燕起秋菰。
樓托難高臥，　饑寒迫向隅。　寂寥相煦沫，
浩蕩報恩珠。　溟漲鯨波動，　衡陽雁影徂。

南征問懸榻，東逝想乘桴。濫竊商歌聽。
時憂卜泣誅。經過憶鄭驛，斟酌旅情孤。

In my Boat, I Set out from the Southern Bank of Jiangling; Respectfully Sent to Vice Governor Zheng Shen

Where shall I go next?
From this town, a drifter's trip I make.
My form goes basically with Earth and Wood.
I sail again on river and lake.

Negative, evil energy entangles our society.
Wars sent this old scholar away.
My life, even if a hundred, is like trash.
I meet roadblocks wherever I stay.

Sand is level and clean under rain.
The broad winding shore is seamless with
   the skies.
Chirping crickets follow drifting twigs.
In fall, from wild rice stalks swallows rise.

It is hard to rest at ease as a wanderer.
I missed my chances, starved and chilled.
In solitude, I get support from friends.
Repaying their huge kindness will be fully
   fulfilled.

Giant waves like whales move in the flooded
sea.
Beyond Hengyang, the sight of wild geese
has always ceased.
In my southern trip, I seek one who can
recognize my talent,
Imagining myself on a magic raft heading
east.

At times, I worry about my hidden worth and
similar fate with Bian.
Someone sang a mournful song to impress a
duke in history, but I fail.
I recall Zheng and his free lodges for guests,
on my way.
In my lonely journey, I have been cheered by
our shared ale.

泊岳陽城下

江國踰千里，山城近百層。岸風翻夕浪，
舟雪灑寒燈。留滯才難盡，艱危氣益增。
圖南未可料，變化有鯤鵬。

Mooring below Yueyang City

I passed a thousand miles on lake and land.
This hillside town is about a hundred stories
  in height.
My boat's cold lamp is under a spray of snow.
Winds from the shore make waves at night.
Detained, I find it hard to use my talent fully.
In hardship, I show more fight.
Like the kun and roc, with ventures ahead,
I have not scheduled my southbound trip tight.

移居公安敬贈衛大郎鈞

衛侯不易得，　予病汝知之。　雅量涵高遠，
清襟照等夷。　平生感意氣，　少小愛文辭。
河海由來合，　風雲若有期。　形容勞宇宙，
質樸謝軒墀。　自古幽人泣，　流年壯士悲。
水煙通徑草，　秋露接園葵。　入邑狠狼鬥，
傷弓鳥雀飢。　白頭供宴語，　烏几伴棲遲。
交態遭輕薄，　今朝豁所思。

Moving to Gongan; Respectfully Presented to Wei Jun, the First

Lord Wei is a rare breed.

About my illness, with care you know.
Your broad mind comes from a lofty nature.
To all, your leniency and kindness go.

All you life, you act from your heart.
A lover of literature, since youth you want to
    write.
River and sea always meet.
Wind and cloud at times unite.

My worn look is from toiling all over.
I decline visits to grand mansions, being
    simple and plain.
Since ancient times, recluses have wept.
People in their prime grieve as years wane.

Mist over waters passes through a grassy path.
In my yard, autumn dew stays on mallows.
Like jackal and wolf, rebels fight into the city.
Hungry birds get wounded by bows.

White-haired, I make time for feasts and talks.
As a detained wanderer, my companion is a
    small black tray.
Some acquaintances have given me slight.
My thoughts get reconciled today.

別董頲

窮冬急風水，逆浪開帆難。士子甘旨闕，
不知道里寒。有求彼樂土，南適小長安。
到我舟檝去，覺君衣裳單。素聞趙公節，
兼盡賓主歡。已結門樓望，無令霜雪殘。
老夫纜已解，脫粟朝未餐。飄蕩兵甲際，
幾時懷抱寬。漢陽頗寧靜，峴首試考槃。
當念著白帽，采薇青雲端。

Parting from Dong Ting

Under strong wind and wave, at winter's end,
Setting sail is hard against the current.
Scholars have no idea how cold the road is,
Even though glad to be at the gate for royal
    decrees sent.

You head south for "Little Changan".
To seek a happy land, you probe.
When you came to my small boat,
I was aware of your thin robe.

I have often heard of the principles of Lord
    Zhao.
You will experience his hospitality in a full
    share.

Already your family watches for your return.
Do not wait until frost and snow are not there.

This old man has loosened his moorings,
Without eating his coarse breakfast.
Wandering at the edge of warfare,
From my mind, when will I get worries past?

At Mount Xian, I shall try to be a recluse.
Hangyang is quite peaceful and quiet.
My wearing a white hat and picking vetches
　　by blue clouds
Should be the image that your mind will get.

清明二首，其一

朝來新火起新煙，湖色春光淨客船。繡羽
銜花他自得，紅顏騎竹我無緣。胡童結束
還難有，楚女腰肢亦可憐。不見定王城舊
處，長懷賈傅井依然。虛沾周舉為寒食，
實借嚴君賣卜錢。鐘鼎山林各天性，濁醪
粗飯任吾年。

The Qingming Festival, no.1

In a clean passenger boat on a sunlit lake in

spring,
Dawn cooking fire and smoke rise anew.
A bird with brocade feathers holds a bloom
at ease.
Fate did not pair me up with a girl on a horse
made of bamboo.
Costumes of nomad lads are rare finds.
Adorable waists go with ladies of Chu.
The well of Tutor Jia is long in my memory.
The site of the old city of Prince of Ding is
not in view.
The shorter Cold food Festival done by Zhou
Ju was a virtual gain.
My fortune-telling in Chengdu on credit is
true.
The rich and hermits act according to their
nature.
Let me live out my years with coarse meals
and unfiltered brew.

清明二首，其二

此身飄泊苦西東，右臂偏枯半耳聾。寂寂
繫舟雙下淚，悠悠伏枕左書空。十年蹴鞠
習俗同。旅雁上雲歸紫塞，家人鑽火用青

楓。秦城樓閣煙花裏，漢主山河錦繡中。
風水春來洞庭闊，白蘋愁殺白頭翁。

The Qingming Festival, no.2

To east and west, my painful wanderings
spread,
With my right arm partly numb and ears
half-dead.
Quietly I tie my boat in tears.
Freely prostrating on my pillow, I write with
my left hand overhead.
For myriad miles, the custom of playing on
swings is the same.
For ten years, I have sent afar my football-
kicking, young lad.
Migratory wild geese in the clouds return to
the purple frontiers.
Green maples used by householders in
drilling for fire are not dead.
Towers and pavilions of the capital stand
amid mist and bloom.
In spring, wind and water of Lake Dongting
look widespread.
Hills and rivers of our empire resemble
brocade and embroidery.
White duckweeds make this white-haired
man extremely sad.

2:

POEMS NOT IN CHRONOLOGY

****

陪章留後惠義寺餞嘉州崔都督赴州

中軍待上客，　令肅事有恆。　前驅入寶地，
祖帳飄金繩。　南陌既留歡，　茲山亦深登。
清聞樹杪磬，　遠謁雲端僧。　迴策匪新岸，
所攀仍舊藤。　耳激洞門飆，　目存寒谷冰。
出塵閟軌躅，　畢景遺炎蒸。　永願坐長夏，
將衰棲大乘。　羈旅惜宴會，　艱難懷友朋。
勞生共幾何，　離恨兼相仍。

271

Accompanying Deputy Zhang Holding a Parting Feast in Huiyi Temple for Commander Cui of Jiazhou as he Sets out for his Prefecture

The Central Command entertains an
    important guest,
With regular procedures done seriously and
    to the full extent.
The outriders enter the precious temple
    grounds.
Fluttering golden cords mark the grand tent.

We climb a hill for its depth and height.
After lingering in joy on the south pathway,
We hear clearly the chimes over treetops
And have an audience with a monk far away.

Our returning route is not towards a new bank.
We climb using the same vines still.
There is an earful of blasts near caves.
Of the cold valley's ice, our eyes have their
    fill.

Away from the dust of life and without
    faltering in a rut,
We leave behind steamy heat on a day of
    sunlight.

I wish to let my frail body sit all summer
And my mind rest on Mahayana Buddhism's
   insight.

I value feasts as a detained wanderer
And think of friends in my difficult days.
How much longer can my belabored life last?
With me, my parting regret always stays.

又於韋處乞大邑瓷碗

大邑燒瓷輕且堅，扣如哀玉錦城傳。君家
白碗勝霜雪，急送茅齋也可憐。

Also Asking Wei for Porcelain Bowls from Dayi

The porcelains fired at Dayi are light but hard
   in every way.
Knocked, the sad tone seems to be from jade
   pegs, people of Brocade City say.
The bowls of your household are whiter than
   snow.
Send such lovely objects to my thatched
   study without delay.

又送

雙峰寂寂對春台，萬竹青青照客杯。細草
留連侵室軟，殘花帳望近人開。同舟昨日
何由得，並馬今朝未擬廻。直到綿州始分
手，江邊樹裏共誰來。

Another on Parting

Facing the spring terrace, twin peaks still
  look lonesome.
Countless green bamboos reflect in the
  parting cup of my guest.
As I linger, I find soft invasive grass indoors.
While I look and sulk, near me late flowers
  blossom.
Sharing a boat with you the other day was
  not possible.
On horseback side by side today, I put plans
  of returning to rest.
It will be at Mianzhou that we shall begin to
  part.
To my riverside abode among trees, with
  whom can I come?

重題鄭氏東亭

華亭入翠微，秋日亂清暉。崩石敧山樹，
清漣曳水衣。紫鱗衝岸躍，蒼隼護巢歸。
向晚尋征路，殘雲傍馬飛。

Another Inscription on Master Zheng 's East Pavilion

This grand pavilion blends with verdant hills.
The fall sun emits a cool glow in disarray.
Clear ripples drag sheets of algae.
By cracked rocks, hillside trees are pressed.
A purple fish jumps up towards the shore.
A gray falcon returns to guard its nest.
With my horse flying through residual clouds,
By evening, for my next leg, I seek the way.

假山

序：天寶初，南曹小司寇舅於我太夫人堂
下壘土為山，一匱盈尺，以代彼朽木，承
諸焚香瓷甌，甌甚安矣。旁植慈竹，蓋茲
數峰，嶔岑嬋娟，宛有塵外致，乃不知興
之所至，而作是詩。

一匱功盈尺，三峰意出群。望中疑在野，
幽處欲生雲。慈竹春陰覆，香爐曉勢分。
惟南將獻壽，佳氣日氛氳。

Artificial Mountain

Preface:　At the beginning of the Tianbo era (742-756), my maternal uncle, Vice-Director of the Department of Criminal Justice, piled earth into a mountain by the hall of my grandmother. From a basketful of soil was formed an artificial mountain just over a foot high, to replace the dead wooden base of an incense burner stand, which can hold porcelain incense bowls securely. Beside it, he planted some gentle bamboos which can cover several peaks. The lofty ridges and graceful charm of bamboos offer a mood beyond this world. I got carried away by the inspiration aroused and wrote this poem.

From a basketful of soil is formed a full foot
　　of an artificial mountain.
In spirituality, its three peaks can excel.
Clouds are about to emerge from quiet spots.
I seem to be in the wilds, as I gaze.
Gentle bamboos offer shade in spring.
At dawn, its lay on an incense burner stand

shows well.

There is a daily emission of auspicious energy.

Like South Mountain, it is a proper gift for celebrating birthdays.

夜聽許十誦詩愛而有作

許生五台賓，　業白出石壁。　予亦師粲可，
身猶縛禪寂。　何階子方便，　謬引為匹敵。
離索晚相逢，　包蒙欣有擊。　誦詩渾遊衍，
四座皆辟易。　應手看捶鈎，　清心聽鳴鏑。
精微穿溟涬，　飛動摧霹靂。　陶謝不枝梧，
風騷共推激。　紫燕自超詣，　翠駁誰剪剔。
君意人莫知，　人間夜寥闃。

At Night, after Listening to Xu, the Tenth, Chant Poems, I Write in Appreciation

Master Xu, a resident in a temple of Mount Wutai

Left Stone Cliff after lessons were done.

I also followed Sengcan and Huite as my teachers

Though still tied to "Silent Illumination

Meditation", for one.

How can I rise to your level in the Buddhist
	Logic of Convenience?
People mistake us as rivals in fight.
Alone and forlorn, I meet you late in life.
Your lifting me from ignorance gives me
	delight.

Everyone present recoils in amazement
When your easy style of chanting shows.
It is smooth and natural,
Like a clear mind listening to ringing arrows.

Your deep sentiments can pierce the primal
	chaos
And smash thunderstorms in quick motion.
Like Tao and Xie, your skill is varied
	and specialized.
Like ancient airs and Li Sao, your poems
	stir the audience with emotion.

Like Purple Swallow, the rare steed, your
	aptitude excels.
Like Dark Dapple, the mixed breed, your
	grooming is just right.
Your thoughts are unknown to earthlings,
On this quiet, desolate night.

中夜

中夜江山靜， 危樓望北辰。 長為萬里客，
有愧百年身。 故國風雲氣， 高堂戰伐塵。
胡雛負恩澤， 嗟爾太平人。

At Midnight

I look at the Pole Star from a tall tower.
At midnight, river and hill are quiet.
I am shamed that at the age of fifty,
On a long course as a wanderer, I am set.
The dust of warfare lands on high halls.
By the vigor of political change, stability
   in my homeland is upset.
An Lushan, the nomad chick, betrayed our
   king's kindness.
I sigh for the peace our people fail to get.

鄭駙馬池台喜遇鄭廣文同飲

不謂生戎馬， 何知共酒杯。 燃臍郿塢敗，
握節漢臣回。 白髮千莖雪， 丹心一寸灰。
別離經死地， 披寫忽登臺。 重對秦簫發，
俱過阮宅來。 留連春夜舞， 淚落強徘徊。

At the Pond and Terrace of Prince Consort Zheng, Happy to Meet Instructor Zheng and Drink with him

I never thought I would live among
    warhorses.
About drinking wine together, I have yet to
    know.
Like the loyal Han envoy, Instructor Zheng
    returned with our king's standards.
Like a dead rebel with his navel lit at Mei,
    An Lushan is our defeated foe.
My patriotic heart can burn down to one
    inch of ash.
My white hair resembles a thousand strands
    of snow.
Parted, we passed through areas with war
    casualties,
Suddenly we climb a terrace, with poems to
    follow.
Once again like Xiaoshi, the Prince Consort
    plays on the flute.
Two Zhengs resemble two Ruans as
    neighbors long ago.
We linger and dance at night in spring.
Teary, we force ourselves to pace to and fro.

秋笛

清商欲盡奏，奏苦血沾衣。他日傷心極，
征人白骨歸。相逢恐恨過，故作發聲微。
不見秋雲動，悲風稍稍飛。

Autumn Flute

I wish to make the shang tone as hard as I can.
Blood stains my robe when I strike the chords
    all the way.
Soldiers on expeditions may return as white
    bones.
It will utterly break my heart on a future day.
Not to meet again is my regret.
To voice my mind, on purpose softly I play.
With a cheerless wind slightly moving,
In a motionless state, fall clouds stay.

蘇端薛復筵簡薛華醉歌

文章有神交有道，端復得之名譽早。愛客
滿堂盡豪翰，開筵上日思芳草。安得健步
移遠梅，亂插繁花向晴昊。千里猶殘舊冰
雪，百壺且試開懷抱。垂老惡聞戰鼓悲，
急觴為緩憂心擣。少年努力縱談笑，看我

281

形容已枯槁。座中薛華善醉歌，歌詞自作風格老。近來海內為長句，汝與山東李白好。何劉沈謝力未工，才兼鮑照愁絕倒。諸生頗盡新知樂，萬事終傷不自保。

氣酣日落西風來，願吹野水添金杯。如澠之酒常快意，亦知窮愁安在哉。忽憶雨時秋井塌，古人白骨生青苔。如何不飲令心哀。

At the Feast of Su Duan and Xue Fu, a Song of Drunkenness as a Note to Xue Hua

With divinely inspired writings, you build
  friendships according to the Way.
Duan and Fu have got fame without delay.
Cherished guests, in a full hall, are all bold
  men of letters.
They long for frequent herbs in a feast on an
  important day.
At random, dense flowers are pinned as we
  face the sun.
How can one hurry to transplant plum blooms
  far away?
Old ice and snow still remain for endless
  miles.
Let us try out the countless pots of wine, for

fun and play.

Getting old, I hate to hear war-drums in grief.

Passing cups fast helps to hold my worries in
delay.

Young people try hard to indulge in chatters
and laughter.

See my already withered look today.

Xue Hua in the feast is good at songs of
drunkenness.

In his lyrics, maturity of style shows.

Of late, within the four seas, you make poems
in the long line format.

To you and Li Bai of Shandong, the same
positive recognition goes.

He, Liu, Shen and Xie lack skills in the
long line format.

In ability, you match Bao Zhao, known for
his melancholy in the past.

Here, we all fully enjoy meeting new friends,

But will eventually get saddened since
nothing can last.

At sunset, drunk and indulged, as west winds
blow.

I hope to add water in nature to our golden
cups,

Like that from River Sheng, always satisfying.

My extreme grief will disappear, I know.

Suddenly I recall how wells cave in during
    fall rain.
Green moss grows on white bones of ancients.
How can I quit drinking and be in sorrow?

鄭駙馬宅宴洞中

主家陰洞細煙霧，留客夏簟青琅玕。春酒
杯濃琥珀薄，冰漿碗碧瑪瑙寒。誤疑茅堂
過江麓，已入風磴霾雲端。自是秦樓壓鄭
谷，時聞雜佩聲珊珊。

At the House of Prince Consort Zheng, Feasting in the Grotto

The host's dark grotto is rather misty.
Summer mats for guests staying over are of
    green bamboo.
Like cold agate, emerald bowls of wine
    taste icy.
Into thin amber cups go strong spring brew.
I am already on windy rocky steps at the
    brim of thick clouds.
My bet on the thatched hall beyond riverside
    foothills is undue.
With the tinkling of mixed pendants in your

ears,
A palace tower naturally beats hermit
    Zheng's grotto in value.

悲秋

涼風動萬里，　群盜尚縱橫。　家遠傳書日，
秋來為客情。　秋窺高鳥過，　老逐衆人行。
始欲投三峽，　何由見兩京。

Autumn Lament

A cold wind blows from endless miles away.
Like thieves, all over rebels still engage us in
    fight.
Today, as I send a letter to my home afar,
The coming of fall puts me in a wanderer's
    plight.
I follow the crowd, traveling as an old man
And watching passing birds in fall at a height.
My initial wish was seeking refuge in the
    Three Gorges.
How can I keep the two capitals in sight?

苦戰行

苦戰身死馬將軍，自云伏波之子孫。干戈
未定失壯士，使我歎恨傷精魂。去年江南
討狂賊，臨江把臂難再得。別時孤雲今不
飛，時獨看雲淚橫臆。

Ballad of Bitter Fighting

He claimed to be the heir of the "Wave
    Quelling General".
General Ma died after a bitter fight.
With my spirit wounded, I sigh with regret,
For losing a brave man in unsettled warfare.
It is hard to clasp his arm by the river again.
To rid a mad rebel, he was in South of the
    River last year.
I often watch clouds alone with tears on my
    chest.
You are the lone cloud I parted from, now no
    more in flight.

與鄠縣源大少府宴渼陂(得寒字)

應為西陂好，金錢罄一餐。飯炒雲子白，
瓜嚼水精寒。無計囘船下，空愁避酒難。
主人情爛熳，持答翠琅玕。

Banquet at Meipi with Yuan Senior, District Defender of Hu County (my Allotted Word is "Cold")

It must be due to the fine lake in the west
That on a single meal, you used up your gold.
I take in rice, cloud-like and white
And chew on melons, crystalline and cold.
Without a plan to return to the boat,
I worry only about my abstinence to uphold.
Let me present this poem to answer yours,
    like rare jade.
My host's kind sentiments brilliantly unfold.

崔駙馬山亭宴集

蕭史幽棲地，林閒蹋鳳毛。沋流何處入，
亂石閉門高。客醉揮金碗，詩成得繡袍。
清秋多宴會，終日困香醪。

287

Banquet at the Hillside Pavilion of Prince Consort Cui

This is where Xiao Shi lived as a recluse.
A transcendent can tread phoenix feathers
   in the grove.
Where does the undercurrent enter?
Your gate is hidden by jumbled rocks above.
Drunk guests raise their golden cups to drink,
Each to get an embroidered robe when poetry
   writing is through.
In clear autumn, banquets number many.
All day long, I am trapped by frequent brew.

苦竹

青冥亦自守，軟弱強扶持。味苦夏蟲避，
叢卑春鳥疑。軒墀曾不重，剪伐欲無辭。
幸近幽人屋，霜根結在茲。

Bitter Bamboos

Soft and weak, they struggle to gain support,
Standing on their own, by day and night.
Summer insects avoid them for their bitter
   taste.
Birds do not trust their low clumps in spring.

They quietly let themselves be chopped,
Never valued for porches with a good height.
By chance, near a recluse's hut,
To the soil there, their frosty roots may cling.

水會渡

山行有常程，　中夜尚未安。　微月沒已久，
崖傾路何難。　大江動我前，　淘若溟渤寬。
篙師暗理楫，　歌笑輕波瀾。　霜濃木石滑，
風急手足寒。　入舟已千憂，　陟巘仍萬盤。
回眺積水外，　始知眾星乾。　遠遊令人瘦，
衰疾慚加餐。

Converging Waters Crossing

With a regular schedule on my hike,
I have yet to find lodging by midnight.
How hard the trip is by a slanting cliff!
The faint moon is long out of sight.

The big river runs before me,
Like the broad, dark sea, scouring with might.
Singing and laughing, a boatman rows in the
  dark.
On waves, he puts a slight.

Trees and rocks get slick in the dense frost.
My limbs feel cold in a blast.
Entering the boat, I already had much worry.
Myriad turns stay near the peak, as in the past.

Peering back over the dense mass of waters,
I begin to sense the sharpness of each star.
With shame, I eat more though frail and sick.
My thin body is the result of traveling afar.

渡江

春江不可渡，二月已風濤。舟楫欹斜疾，
魚龍偃臥高。渚花張素錦，汀草亂青袍。
戲問垂綸客，悠悠見汝曹。

Crossing the River

The river in spring cannot be crossed.
In the second month, waves already rise from
   a blast.
Fish and dragon ride high, lying flat.
Oars held aslant move boats fast.
Flowers on sandbars spread like sheets of
   white brocade.

For green robes, grass on the shore can
    be passed.
When I see anglers so leisurely for so long,
I playfully ask of those with their fishing
    lines cast.

即事

聞道花門破，和親事卻非。人憐漢公主，
生得渡河歸。秋思抛雲鬢，腰支膡寶衣。
群凶猶索戰，回首意多違。

Current Events

The marriage alliance did not work.
Our Uigher allies from Huamen were crushed,
    from hearsay I know.
People pity the Chinese princess,
Who crossed the river for home, after being
    let go.
Her precious robe looks too large for her
    wasted waist and limbs.
She lets loose her cloud-like hair knot, sunk
    in thoughts of sorrow.
Ferocious rebels are still warlike.
In retrospect, expected results do not always

follow.

殿中楊監見示張旭草畫圖

斯人已云死，草聖秘難得。及茲煩見示，
滿目一淒惻。萬里起古色。鏘鏘鳴玉動，
落落群松直。連山蟠其間，溟漲與筆力。
有練實先書，臨池真畫墨。俊拔為之主，
暮年思轉極。未知張王後，誰並百代則。
嗚呼東吳精，逸氣感清識。楊公拂篋笥，
舒卷忘寢食。念昔揮毫端，不獨觀酒德。

Director Yang of the Palace Shows me a Scroll of Zhang Xu's Calligraphy in Cursive Script

That man has already died.
The secret of the sage of the cursive script
  is hard to obtain.
Now that someone takes the trouble to show
  his work,
I feel sad for the full view I can gain.

A faint, cheerless wind emerges from the silk,
With the pigment of antiquity coming from
  endless miles away.

Clang, clang goes flipping brush strokes like
  jade chimes.
Like vertical pines, far-spaced, straight lines
  make an array.

His calligraphy presents the image of coiled,
  linked hills,
With strokes creating energy equal to that
  of a flood at sea.
The brush that wrote on anything, preferably
  silk,
Could blacken a pond when washed, owned
  by Zhang Zhi.

He topped all talented calligraphers,
With extreme thoughts as aging went on from
  its onset.
I know not, after Zhang Zhi and Wang Xizhi,
Who can match the time-honored standard set.

O death, this excellent man from East Wu
Shared his refined disposition and clear
  insight.
Mister Yang wipes and cleans his bamboo
  chest.
Before the unrolled scrolls, forgetting to eat
  and sleep is alright.
When we recall how Zhang Xu wielded his

brush-tips in the past,
The benefit of wine is not the only factor in
  our sight.

楊監又出畫鷹十二扇

近時馮紹正，　能畫鷙鳥樣，　明公出此圖，
無乃傳其狀。　殊姿各獨立，　清絕心有向。
疾禁千里馬，　氣敵萬人將。　憶昔驪山宮，
冬移含元仗。　天寒大羽獵，　此物神俱王。
當時無凡材，　百中皆用壯。　粉墨形似閒，
識者一惆悵。　干戈少暇日，　真骨老崖嶂。
為君除狡兔，　會是翻鞲上。

Director Yang Further Brings out Paintings of Falcons in Twelve Panels

Of late, Feng Shaozheng
Aptly painted the likeness of birds of prey.
These paintings that Your Honor brought out
Only let their shapes and sizes be in display.
Their unique manners clearly reflect their
  different minds.
Each bird poses in its own way.
Compared with top generals and rare steeds,
The speed and energy of the falcons can

294

outplay.

I recall how in winter the guards of Hanyuan
    Hall

Moved to the Palace of Mount Li yesterday.

These creatures dominated in vigor,

In a grand hunt, on a cold day.

Back then, there were no mediocre talents.

All commissioned painters could do better
    than the rest.

If pigments could lend a semblance of form,

All connoisseurs would feel depressed.

Leisure is rare during warfare.

On cliffs and mountain barriers, true birds
    can age and stay.

A falcon will return to its master's gauntlet,

Once it has helped him put cunning hares
    away.

獨酌成詩

燈花何太喜，酒綠正相親。醉裏從為客，
詩成覺有神。兵戈猶在眼，儒術豈謀身。
苦被微官縛，低頭愧野人。

Drinking Wine Alone and Completing a Poem

Why do lamp sparks make people glad?
I feel just cozy with green wine.
When drunk, I accept being a wanderer.
Finished poems give me energy, lifting and
    divine.
How can one live on a scholar's skill?
Warfare is still before our eyes.
In shame, I lower my head before rustics,
Suffering from being stuck in a minor post
    with its ties.

遣懷

愁眼看霜露，寒城菊自花。天風隨斷柳，
客淚墮清笳。水靜樓陰直，山昏塞日斜。
夜來歸鳥盡，啼殺後棲鴉。

Expressing my Mind

In the cold city, chrysanthemums naturally
    bloom.
To frost and dew, in sorrow my vision goes.
A wanderer tears from sharp reed flute notes.
Winds from the sky take off with broken

twigs of willows.
Frontier sunbeams fall aslant on dim hills.
On still waters fall the tower's straight
  shadows.
Birds have all returned by night.
The screech is deafening at late-roosting
  crows.

太平寺泉眼

招提憑高岡，　疏散連草莽。　出泉枯柳根，
汲引歲月古。　石閒見海眼，　天畔縈水府。
廣深丈尺閒，　宴息敢輕侮。　青白二小蛇，
幽姿可時睹。　如絲氣或上，　爛熳為雲雨。
山頭到山下，　鑿井不盡土。　取供十方僧，
香美勝牛乳。　北風起寒文，　弱藻舒翠縷。
明涵客衣淨，　細蕩林影趣。　何當宅下流，
餘潤通藥圃。　三春濕黃精，　一食生毛羽。

The Fountainhead at Taiping Temple

On a high hill, the monastery is set,
With scattered buildings joined by a thicket.
A spring emerges from the roots of a dead
  willow.
They have drawn water from it since ages ago.

Among rocks are seen springs called "Eyes
    of the Sea".
Towards the horizon, the massive rippled
    waters flow,
In depth and width about a yard,
Not to be underestimated without a billow.
Two little snakes, green and white,
In a still state, at times remain.
Like silk, evaporation may rise,
Swollen as cloud and rain.
Up and down the hill,
Dry wells all lead to the dry ground.
The spring water is drawn and used by
    countless monks.
Sweeter than the milk of cows, it is found.
The north wind creates cold ripples.
Weak algae spread their threads in green.
Small undulations liven up the forest.
The limpidity makes my robe look clean.
How can I build my house downstream,
With the surplus moisture passing my herb
    garden freely?
My well-watered herb, Huang Jing, through
    spring,
Will be my quick elixir to be a fairy.

望岳

西嶽崚嶒竦處尊，諸峰羅立如兒孫。安得
仙人九結杖，拄到玉女洗頭盤。車箱入谷
無歸路，箭栝通天有一門。稍待西風涼冷
後，高尋白帝問真源。

Gazing at a High Mountain

The west summit is steep and fearful at a
   height.
Like children and grandchildren, the many
   peaks are aligned right.
How can I get the nine-section staff of a fairy
For a prop to reach Jade Maidens' Hair
   Washing Basin on site?
There is no returning route for my cart
   inside the valley,
Except a gate open to the sky for arrows to
   shoot through.
I shall wait until the cool west wind comes
Before I seek out White Emperor on high，
   for the source of All True.

得房公池鵝

房相西亭鵝一群，眠沙泛浦白如雲。鳳凰
池上應廻首，為報籠隨王右軍。

Getting a Goose from Lord Fang's Pool

To sleep on the sand by Lord Fang's West
  Pavilion, flocked geese go.
Whiter than clouds, they float near the shore
  to and fro.
The one for me must be like that turning its
  head by Phoenix Pond.
The barter Wang Xizhi made on a caged
  goose is what I shall follow.

垂白

垂白馮唐老，清秋宋玉悲。江喧長少睡，
樓廻獨移時。多難身何補，無家病不辭。
甘從千日醉，未許七哀詩。

Hanging White

With hanging white hair, Feng Tang aged.
In clear autumn, Song Yu was in sorrow.

I sleep little for long by a noisy river.
Alone I pass time in a tower, out of the way.
With much turmoil, what help can I offer?
With a homeless man, many illnesses stay.
I would gladly spend countless days drunk,
Not qualified to write the famed "Poems on
    Seven Sources of Sorrow".

聞斛斯六官未歸

故人南郡去，去索作碑錢。本賣文為活，
翻令室倒懸。荊扉深蔓草，土銼冷疏煙。
老罷休無賴，歸來省醉眠。

Hearing that the Official Husi, the Sixth, has not Returned

To seek money for writing stele inscriptions,
He left for South County, a friend from the
    days of old.
In contrast, his livelihood turned upside down.
Originally he tried to earn enough with his
    writings sold.
His humble gate is deep in weeds.
With infrequent smoke, his earthenware pan
    is cold.

On return, drink yourself to sleep less often.
Already aged, stop acting reckless and bold.

不見

不見李生久，佯狂真可哀。世人皆欲殺，
吾意獨憐才。敏捷詩千首，飄零酒一杯。
匡山讀書處，頭白好歸來。

I have not Seen

Long I have not seen Li Bai.
It is really lamentable that you pretended to
  be insane.
All earthlings want to kill you,
But a will to appreciate your talent alone, I
  maintain.
Your quick wit produced endless poems.
A cup of wine is what a wanderer can gain.
From Kuang Hill where you studied,
With a head of white hair, please come again.

兩當縣吳十侍禦江上宅

I

寒城朝煙澹，山谷落葉赤。陰風千里來，
吹汝江上宅。鶺雞號枉渚，日色傍阡陌。
借問持斧翁，幾年長沙客。哀哀失木狖，
矯矯避弓翮。亦知故鄉樂，未敢思宿昔。
昔在鳳翔都，共通金閨籍。天子猶蒙塵，
東郊暗長戟。

II

兵家忌聞諜，此輩常接跡。臺中領舉劾，
君必慎剖析。不忍殺無辜，所以分白黑。
上官擁許與，失意見遷斥。仲尼甘旅人，
向子識損益。朝廷非不知，閉口休歎息。
予時忝錚臣，丹陛實咫尺。相愛受狼狽，
至死難塞責。行邁心多違，出門無與適，
惆悵頭更白，於公負明義。

The House by the River of Attendant Censor Wu, the Tenth, in Liangdong County

I

Leaves dropping into valleys look red.
In the cold city, a pale dawn mist shows.
Onto your house by the river,
From endless miles away, a ghastly wind
  blows.

Sunlight falls on paths between fields.
At a sandbar, a wronged phoenix cries.
May I ask a faulted and condemned old man:
How many years as a wanderer in Changsha
  he lies?

Your strong wings dodge arrows.
A monkey grieves over missing its tree.
You do not know the joy of being home
And dare not recall how it used to be.

In the capital at Fengxiang, in the past,
We were on the golden roster of the palace.
The Son of Heaven was still a refugee.
The east outskirts were darkened by wars in
  place.

II

Those in the military hate spies.
Rebels come on end most everywhere.
The censor deals with all impeachments.
You always dissect and analyze for truth
    with care.

Striving to separate right from wrong,
You cannot bear to kill the innocent.
High officials first approved of you.
Then, out of favor, to exile you were sent.

Changzi could tell between gain and loss.
With his teachings, Confucius was glad to ply.
Not that the palace was ignorant of your case,
But those who knew you did not talk or sigh.

I was then a remonstrating officer.
The throne was actually a foot away.
I saw your wretched state.
All my life, my guilt for not helping will stay.

On this long trip, I feel mostly amiss
And leaving your door, nothing is right.
I have owed you openness and justice.
Depressed, I find more hair turning white.

從人覓小猢猻許寄

人說南州路，山猿樹樹懸。舉家聞若駭，
為寄小如拳。預哂愁胡面，初調見馬鞭。
許求聰慧者，童稚捧應癲。

I was Looking for a Small Monkey and Someone Promised to Send One to me

They say on the roads in the south counties,
By hills, monkeys hang from every tree.
Hearing this, my whole family was shocked.
A small one, like a fist, will be sent to me.
I expect smiling at its face like a sad nomad.
A trainer's horse-whip is the first it will see.
I hope for a clever one.
Holding it, my children should go crazy.

和裴迪登新津寺寄王侍郎

何限倚山木，吟詩秋葉黃。蟬聲集古寺，
鳥影度寒塘。風物悲遊子，登臨憶侍郎。
老夫貪佛日，隨意宿僧房。

306

In Answer to the Poem of Pei Di: "Climbing to Xinjin Temple", Sent to Deputy Director Wang

We can endlessly lean against hillside trees
And chant poems as fall leaves turn yellow.
The old temple is a hub for buzzing cicadas.
Across a cold pool, reflections of birds go.
I recall the deputy director, after climbing.
To a wanderer, the scenery brings sorrow.
This old man craves Buddha Day.
My wish to stay overnight in the monk's cell
   I follow.

陪李七司馬皂江上觀造竹橋即日成往來之
人免冬寒入水聊題短作簡李公二首，其一

伐竹為橋結構同，褰裳不涉往來通。天寒
白鶴歸華表，日落青袍見水中。顧我老非
題柱客，知君才是濟川功。合歡卻笑千年
事，驅石何時到海東。

In the Company of Adjutant Li, the Seventh, by Black River, we Survey the Construction of a Bamboo Bridge Completed that Very Day, so Travelers can Avoid Wading in the Winter's Cold. I Chance to Write Two Short Poems for Li, no.1

Bridge construction is the same for wood or
   bamboo.
No wading is needed; the traffic is through.
In the cold, white cranes return to the Grand
   Pillar by a bridge.
At sunset, in mid-stream, green dragons come
   in view.
I am too old to inscribe on a bridge to vow
   my future success.
The merit of bridging a river is for you.
All cheered, we mock at the Qin king myriad
   years ago.
When did his stone bridge reach the sea's
   east for the sun, after much ado?

陪李七司馬皂江上觀造竹橋即日成往來之
人免冬寒入水聊題短作簡李公二首，其二

把燭成橋夜，回舟坐客時。天高雲去盡，
江廻月來遲。衰謝多扶病，招邀屢有期。
異方乘此興，樂罷不免悲。

**In the Company of Adjutant Li, the
Seventh, by Black River, we Survey the
Construction of a Bamboo Bridge
Completed that Very Day, so Travelers
can Avoid Wading in the Winter's Cold. I
Chance to Write Two Short Poems for Li,
no.2**

Guests sit and sail around in a boat at night,
Holding candles to see the bridge you create.
It is a cloudless, tall sky.
Above the winding stream, the moon is late.
Frequent invitations come my way
Though my sick body is in a waning state.
In a strange land, sharing the fun,
I cannot help feeling sad when joys dissipate.

中宵

西閣百尋餘，中宵望綺疏。飛星過水白，
落月動沙虛。擇木知幽鳥，潛波想巨魚。
親朋滿天地，兵甲少來書。

In the Middle of the Night

In my west pavilion, about a hundred yards
   high,
I gaze at sparse, pretty things at midnight.
Shooting stars are white specks over waters.
At moonset, unmoving sandbanks look tight.
Big fish think about submerging under waves.
Hiding birds know about the right branches
   to stay overnight.
Friends and kin may fill the whole world.
In war, few letters come in sight.

西閣三度期大昌嚴明府同宿不到

問子能來宿，今疑索固要。匣琴虛夜夜，
手板自朝朝。金吼霜鐘澈，花催蠟炬銷。
早鳧江檻底，雙影漫飄飄。

310

In West Pavilion, for the Third Time I Expected Magistrate Yan to Stay over, but he did not Come

I asked if you could come and stay over.
Now if strong requests are useful, I am not
  certain.
Each day you handle cases in your office.
My qin in its case lies idle every night.
The roar of a frosty brazen bell is piercing.
Sparks of a candle hasten it to wane.
Early in the morning, under decks of the river,
Drifting ducks in pairs come in sight.

題鄭縣亭子

鄭縣亭子澗之濱，戶牖憑高發興新。雲斷
岳蓮臨大路，天晴官柳暗長春。巢邊野雀
群欺燕，花底山蜂遠趁人。更欲題詩滿青
竹，晚來幽獨恐傷神。

Inscribed on the Pavilion at Zheng County

By a brook, Zheng County's pavilion gives
  fresh delight,
With windows set at a height.
Clouds break off at Lotus Peak, looking down

on the main road.

In Changchun Palace, sunlit willows cast
their shadows.

Under flowers in the hills, bees chase people
afar.

Wild birds by their nests harass swallows.

What is more, I want to write poems to fill up
green bamboos.

I fear my spirit may hurt, being alone at night.

客舊舘

陳跡隨人事，初秋別此亭。重來梨葉赤，
依舊竹林青。風幔何時卷，寒砧昨夜聲。
無由出江漢，愁緒日冥冥。

Lodging in an Inn where I Stayed before

My former trips followed human, everyday
needs.

From this pavilion in early fall, I went away.

Pear leaves redden on my return.

As before, green bamboo groves stay.

When will the wind-blown drapes be rolled
up?

Mallets in the cold sounded at the end of

yesterday.
Daily I am sunk in a deeper and darker mood.
For me to leave for Yangzi and Han, there is
no way.

述古三首，其一

赤驥頓長纓，非無萬里姿。悲鳴淚至地，
為問馭者誰。鳳凰從天來，何意復高飛。
竹花不結實，念子忍朝饑。古來君臣合，
可以物理推。賢人識其分，進退固其宜。

A Narrative of Ancient Times in Three Poems, no.1

Like a rare horse, a worthy minister stopped
to serve.
It was not due to his inability to persevere.
He questioned the wisdom of the ruler
And sadly spoke out with much tear.
Why does a phoenix again fly off at a height
After from the sky, it wants to appear?
Bamboo flowers bear no fruit.
With daily hunger, a man has to bear.
It is possible to infer from nature's laws.
Since ancient times, the king and his minister

work in a pair.
A sage knows his role in society.
On the right track of life, he wants to fare.

述古三首，其二

市人日中集，於利競錐刀。置膏烈火上，
哀哀自煎熬。農人望歲稔，相率除蓬蒿。
所務穀為本，邪贏無乃勞。舜舉十六相，
身尊道何高。秦時任商鞅，法令如牛毛。

A Narrative of Ancient Times in Three Poems, no.2

Citizens that gather in the day,
For the slightest profit, vie.
Like lard placed on a blazing fire,
They suffer sadly until dry.
Farmers look forward to harvest times.
Team efforts in weeding is what they go by.
Basically they work for grains.
Dishonest gains do not justify.
King Shun used sixteen ministers.
His philosophy was lofty and his prestige
high.
In Qin times, Shang Yang, in his term,

314

Used laws as many as ox hair to make people
   comply.

述古三首，其三

漢光得天下，祚永固有開。豈惟高祖聖，
功自蕭曹來。經綸中興業，何代無長才。
吾慕寇鄧勳。濟時信良哉。耿賈亦宗臣，
羽翼共徘徊。休運終四百，圖畫在雲臺。

A Narrative of Ancient Times in Three Poems, no.3

King Guangwu of Han got all under Heaven.
From the start, lasting blessings did follow.
This was not only due to the sage leadership
   of Gaozu.
To his ministers, Xiao and Cao, credit
   should also go.
In managing the task of restoration,
Which reign lacked great talent?
I admire the legacy of Kou Xun and Deng Yu,
From whom truly good aid for the times was
   sent.
Geng and Jia were honored ministers.
To the king, steady and ready support came.

The dynasty lasted for four hundred years.
Their portraits were on Cloud Terrace to
  mark their fame.

秋日阮隱居致薤三十束

隱者柴門內，畦蔬繞舍秋。盈筐承露薤，
不待致書求。束比青芻色，圓齊玉箸頭。
衰年關鬲冷，味暖併無憂。

On an Autumn Day, Ruan, the Recluse, Sends me Thirty Bundles of Chives

Inside the brushwood gate of the recluse's hut,
In fall, vegetable plots wind around.
A basket full of chives, soaked in dew, comes,
Without a written request from me.
Tied in bundles, they compare well with
  green grass.
Like jade chopsticks, they are trim and round.
My bowels are cold in my waning years.
Warm and mild, this food is worry-free.

九日楊奉先會白水崔明府

今日潘懷縣，同時陸浚儀。坐開桑落酒，
來把菊花枝。天宇清霜淨，公堂宿霧披。
晚酣留客舞，鳧舄共差池。

On the Double Ninth Day, Yang of Fengxian County Meets with Cui, Magistrate of White Water County

Like Pan Yu of Huai county and Lu Yun of
  Junyi County,
Two famous people meet today.
The host sets out fine wine for the season.
The guest holds chrysanthemums in a spray.
The sky is frost-free.
From the public hall, overnight fog lifts at
  he break of day.
The tipsy guest is detained for a dance at
  night,
With wild duck slippers, like those of a fairy,
  in disarray.

重經昭陵

草昧英雄起，謳歌歷數歸。風塵三尺劍，
社稷一戎衣。翼亮貞文德，丕承戢武威。
聖圖天廣大，宗祀日光輝。陵寢盤空曲，
熊羆守翠微。再窺松柏路，還見五雲飛。

Once Again on Passing by Zhaoling

In the chaotic beginning, a hero had his rise.
People sang in praise of each successive reign.
His three-foot sword ended the wind and dust
of wars.
For our state, in his armor he showed fight.
He brilliantly promoted learning and art.
A great successor, he did not rely on might.
Under his sage plan, our broad borders
expanded to the skies.
Ancestral worship was held dear like bright
sunlight.
The mausoleum follows the bend of the
deserted area.
Like bears, brave soldiers guarded the
verdant terrain.
I looked again at the road through pine and
cypress
And the auspicious, five-colored clouds that
scudded as if in flight.

鳳凰台

亭亭鳳凰台，北對西康州。西伯今寂寞，
鳳聲亦悠悠。山峻路絕蹤，石林氣尚浮。
安得萬丈梯，為君上上頭。恐有無母雛，
飢寒日啾啾。我能剖心出，飲啄慰孤愁。
心以當竹實，炯然忘外求。血以當醴泉，
豈徒比清流。所重王者瑞，敢辭微命休。
坐看彩翮長，舉意八極周。自天銜瑞圖，
飛下十二樓。圖以奉為尊，鳳以垂鴻猷。
再光中興業，一洗蒼生憂。深衷正為此，
群盜何淹留。

Phoenix Terrace

Facing West Kangzhou to the north,
The Phoenix Terrace is at a height.
A phoenix came before King Wen of Zhou.
Both are now out of sight.

Mists float among forest-like stone cliffs.
There is no trail to scale the steep hill.
How can I get a long ladder to reach the peak,
For you as I go uphill?

There may be a motherless phoenix
That in hunger and cold, wails all day.

I can cut out my heart for its food and drink
And drive its loneliness away.

My heart is like bamboo seeds
That with self-reliance teem.
My blood is a spring of sweet waters,
Not to be compared with just a clear stream.

Dare I refuse to sacrifice my humble life?
The king's auspiciousness is what we
    emphasize.
Sit and watch its long, colorful feathers.
The mind of the phoenix is on the Eight
    Extremities of the skies.

From Heaven, a phoenix once held an
    auspicious diagram in its beak
And to the Twelve Towers, flew down.
It carried a grand scheme
And presented it to the crown.

Let national revival shine again
And wash the worries of commoners away.
This is from the bottom of my heart.
How can rebels prolong their stay?

戲作寄上漢中王二首，其一

雲裏不聞雙雁過，掌中貪見一珠新。秋風
嫋嫋吹江漢，只在他鄉何處人。

Playful Compositions Sent to the Prince of Hanzhong, no.1

I did not hear two wild geese passing amid
    clouds, with your announcement.
For the new-born son, like a pearl in your
    palm, I crave a view.
The wavering autumn winds blow on Yangzi
    and Han.
Real strangers in a strange land are just too
    few.

戲作寄上漢中王二首，其二

謝安舟楫風還起，梁苑池台雪欲飛。杳杳
東山攜漢妓，泠泠修竹待王歸。

Playful Compositions Sent to the Prince of Hanzhong, no.2

Like Xie An, you calmly watch a rising wind

in your boat.
Like Liang Garden, your pool and terrace can
inspire poets on snow.
You hold the hand of a hired songstress
faintly at East Hill.
Your slender bamboos await the prince's
return as rustling sounds go.

橋陵詩三十韻因呈縣內諸官

I

先帝昔晏駕，茲山朝百靈。崇岡擁象設，
沃野開天庭。即事壯重險，論功超五丁。
披陀因厚地，卻略羅峻屏。雲闕虛冉冉，
風松肅泠泠。石門霜露白，玉殿莓苔青。
宮女晚知曙，祠官朝見星。空梁簇畫戟，
陰井敲銅瓶。中使日夜繼，惟王心不寧。
豈徒恤備享，尚謂求無形。

II

孝理敦國政，神凝推道經。瑞芝產廟柱，
好鳥鳴巖扃。高岳前嵂崒，洪河左瀅濴。
金城蓋峻趾，沙苑交回汀。永與奧區固，

川原紛盼冥。原然赤縣立，臺榭爭岦亭。
官屬果稱是，聲華真可聽。王劉美竹潤，
裴李春蘭馨。鄭氏才振古，唲候筆不停。
遣辭必中律，利物常發硎。

III

綺繡相輾轉，琳琅愈青熒。側聞魯恭化，
秉德崔瑗銘。太史候氜影，王喬隨鶴翎。
朝儀限霄漢，客思廻林坰。轞軻辭下杜，
飄飄陵濁涇。諸生舊短褐，旅泛一浮萍。
荒崴兒女瘦，暮途涕泗零。主人念老馬，
廨署客秋螢。流寓理豈惬，窮愁醉未醒。
何當擺俗累，浩蕩乘蒼溟。

Poem on Qiaoling in Thirty Couplets to be Shown to the Officials of the County

I

When the late king made his last journey,
To pay their respects, a hundred mountain
   spirits came.
Tall ridges provided the likeness of palatial
   layout.
Open, fertile wilds and the heavenly court

looked the same.

The project is both grand and dangerous,
In merit, surpassing the five mountain
    diggers of former years.
The land is of thick earth with slopes,
Slightly screened off by hilly barriers.

The mausoleum blends imperceptibly well
    with clouds.
Past cold, majestic pines, winds get through.
Green lichens and moss grow in jade halls.
On stone gates are white frost and dew.

Lady attendants are late to know of morn.
The staff for sacrifices sees stars at dawn.
A bronze pitcher rattles inside a well in the
    shade.
On empty rafters, clusters of pikes are drawn.

The king finds no peace at heart
Though court messengers ply night and day.
The size of offerings is not the only concern.
Recognition is sought for the dead in a
    spiritual way.

II

With filial piety, he works hard at state affairs,
Promoting Daoism, with a will to concentrate.
Auspicious linghis grow on temple columns.
Fine birds sing out at the cliff by a gate.

A high mountain stands perilously before us.
To its left is a big river, limpid all across.
Here is the ruin of a steep section of the Great
    Wall.
On a sandy park, sandbars crisscross.

It is forever a secret corner of the palace.
All on stream and plain yearn for the night.
It is in all reality a county of its own
Where terrace and arbor vie in height.

The officers here fit their roles,
With their reputation pleasing to the ear,
    with a ring.
Wang and Liu are smooth and tactful like
    fine bamboos.
Pei and Li resemble fragrant orchids in
    spring.

Ages ago, Zheng shocked the world with his
    talent.

In using his brush to write, Count Dan did
  not rest.
His choice of words stays in the middle
  course.
Like a whetstone, he can smoothen anything
  expressed.

III

Rare jade looks greener and clearer in time.
Exquisite embroidery gets passed around.
I sometimes heard about Lu Gong's Rule by
  Enlightenment.
Near Cui Yuan, an inscription on morals was
  always found.

The Grand Astrologer trapped wild ducks and
  got magic slippers.
Wang Qiao, the immortal, left the capital on a
  crane.
Court ceremonies are limited to those
  accessing the Milky Way.
A wanderer thinks of forests and outskirts
  again and again.

In ill-luck and hardship, I left Xiadu.
Crossing muddy River Jing, I got unsettled in
  a boat.

As one of the scholars in an old, homespun
    robe,
In my wanderings, I am a duckweed afloat.

My children grow thin in a famine year.
Waning on the road, I let my tears run free.
When my hosts think of me as an old horse,
Lodging is offered for a fall firefly like me.

How can I go along with living as a wanderer?
In utter sorrow, from drunkenness I am not
    waken.
When can I get off mundane, worldly ties?
On a grand trip to the Dark Seas, let me be
    taken.

官定後戲贈

不作河西尉，淒涼為折腰。老夫怕趨走，
率府且逍遙。耽酒須微祿，狂歌托聖朝。
故山歸興盡，回首向風飆

**Presented in Jest after my Post was
Determined**

In grief, at work I now need to bow to others,

No longer a sheriff of Hexi as in the past.
The job of a military guard is leisurely.
The old man fears running errands fast.
An addict of wine needs a modest salary.
I sing madly; my faith in a sage reign is cast.
Gone is my interest to return home for the
    mountains.
I turn my head and face a blast.

上韋左相二十韻 （見素）

I

鳳曆軒轅紀， 龍飛四十春。 八荒開壽域，
一氣轉洪鈞。 霖雨思賢佐， 丹青憶老臣。
應圖求駿馬， 驚代得麒麟。 沙汰江河濁，
調和鼎鼐新。 韋賢初相漢， 范叔已歸秦。
盛業今如此， 傳經固絕倫。 豫樟深出地，
滄海闊無津。 北斗司喉舌， 東方領搢紳。
持衡留藻鑒， 聽履上星辰。

II

獨步才超古， 餘波德照鄰。 聰明過管輅，
尺牘倒陳遵。 豈是池中物， 由來席上珍。

廟堂知至理，風俗盡還淳。才借俱登用，
愚蒙但隱淪。長卿多病久，子夏索居頻。
回首驅流俗，生涯似衆人。巫咸不可問，
鄒魯莫容身。感激時將晚，蒼茫興有神。
為公歌此曲，涕淚在衣巾。

Presented to Wei Jiansu, Minister of the Left in Twenty Couplets

I

On our phoenix calendar, from Xuanyuan's
   time,
For forty years, you, the dragon, have taken
   flight.
You have dug and mined in the wilds for our
   people,
Turning the Great Potter's Wheel with your
   energy and might.

In heavy rain, the king longed for a worthy
   helper
And recalled an old minister like you, for the
   entire reign.
He should have waited just to find a fine
   steed.
But you are a unicorn of the generation that

329

in awe we could gain.

Like scouring mud from rivers, you weeded
the leaders.
In your new premiership, you led with one
accord.
You are another Wei Xian, Minister of Han
Or Fan Shu who served Qin to mend any
discord.

Such is your grand achievement.
Your success in teaching the classics is
peerless.
Like a camphor tree, you are rooted deep in
the ground.
Like the gray sea, your horizon is broad and
endless.

Like the North Dipper, you are the throat and
tongue of the king.
As the minister of the left, you lead the gentry
class.
You hold fair yardsticks and leave good
evaluations of personnel.
In the palace, people can hear your fairy's
slippers as you pass.

II

In talent, your uniqueness overtakes that of
   ancients.
Your shining virtues have ripple effects on
   those near you.
You are smarter than Guan Lu, the scholar
And can write better letters than Chen Zun,
   in my view.

How can you be a creature trapped in a pool?
That you are always a rare item in a feast
   is sure.
You understand the best guiding principles in
   the courts and halls.
All customs are reverted to be simple and
   pure.

All outstanding talents have been recruited.
Stupid and ignorant, I am in seclusion,
   feeling lost and spent.
Like Sima Xiangru, I have long been sick.
Like Zi Xia, my living in isolation is frequent.

I look back on how I dashed through the
   mundane world.
To a commoner's life, I can relate.
Like Mencius and Confucius, I cannot stay

in my hometown.
I may not ask Shamen Xian of my fate.

I feel emotional as my time is getting late.
In the boundless void, immortals luckily
  exist, to my belief.
I sing this song for Your Honor,
With tears on my robe and kerchief.

雨

行雲遞崇高，　飛雨靄而至。　潺潺石間溜，
汩汩松上駛。　亢陽乘秋熱，　百穀皆已棄。
皇天德澤降，　焦卷有生意。　前雨傷卒暴，
今雨喜容易。　不可無雷霆，　間作鼓增氣。
佳聲達中宵，　所望時一致。　清霜九月天，
髣髴見滯穗。　郊扉及我私，　我圃日蒼翠。
恨無抱甕力，　庶減臨江費。

Rain

As clouds gradually reach a great height,
Flying over will well be a heavy rain.
Slick is the runoff on rocks.
On pines, a rapid stream has lain.

In fall, excessive sunlight brings heat.
Countless crops have been forsaken.
With ethics and kindness, Heaven sent
    downpours.
For the parched and curled plants, a new
    lease of life is taken.

The previous storm hurt us.
The present easy-going rain gladdens me.
We cannot do without occasional thunders
That like drumbeats, can perk our energy.

What I had hoped for in time materialized.
The fine sound arrived at midnight.
Under a sky of clear frost, in the ninth month,
I almost thought ungleaned ears of grain
    came in sight.

It reaches even my private plot outside the
    city.
My garden will get greener every day.
To water my lot using a jug, I hate my lack
    of strength.
To carry water from the river, I shall have
    less to pay.

雨晴

天際秋雲薄，從西萬里風。今朝好晴景，
久雨不妨農。塞柳行疏翠，山梨結小紅。
胡笳樓上發，一雁入高空。

Rain Clears

West winds come from endless miles away.
Thin clouds appear at the horizon in fall.
It is sunny this morning.
Farming is not hurt by prolonged rainfall.
Frontier willows in line look green and sparse.
Hillside pears grow red and small.
A nomad reed pipe sounds from the tower.
A single wild goose enters the sky, cloudless
and tall.

行次鹽亭縣聊題四韻奉寄嚴遂州蓬州兩使

馬首見鹽亭，高山擁縣青，雲溪花淡淡，
春郭水泠泠。金蜀多名士，嚴家聚德星。
長歌意無極，好為老夫聽。

Reaching Yanting County on my Travels, I Chanced to Write Four Couplets, to be Sent Respectfully with a Note to the Yans, Prefects of Suizhou and Pengzhou

Ahead of my horse, I see Yanting County,
Close to the hills, green and towering.
Pale flowers grow by creeks under clouds.
By the city wall, waters run gurgling in
    spring.
There are many celebrated scholars in Shu.
On the Yan family, clusters of stars of virtue
    are shining.
Please lend this old man your ears,
To the long song, with endless thoughts,
    that I sing.

行次昭陵

舊俗疲庸王，　群雄問獨夫。　讖歸龍鳳質，
威定虎狼都。　天屬尊堯典，　神功協禹謨。
風雲隨絕足，　日月繼高衢。　文物多師古，
朝廷半老儒。　直詞寧戮辱，　賢路不崎嶇。
往者災猶降，　蒼生喘未蘇。　指麾安率土，
蕩滌撫洪爐。　將士悲陵邑，　幽人拜鼎湖。

玉衣晨自舉，鐵馬汗常趨。松柏瞻虛殿，
塵沙開國日，流浪滿山隅。

Reaching Zhaoling on my Journey

Old customs wear down inept emperors.
The Sui king, a loner, was confronted by
    heroes.
Omens pointed to one with dragon and
    phoenix qualities,
To exert power at the capital over beast-like
    foes.

A respected model of Yao gave Taizong the
    mandate on the yielded throne.
On Yu's plans, he got Heaven's help to
    succeed.
Sun and moon in turn shine on your imperial
    highway.
Wind and cloud follow his efficiency in
    speed.

Half of his courtiers were old.
Ancient culture was what he followed the
    most.
Those who offered straight counsels were not
    killed or shamed.
It was not a rugged road for a worthy of

ability to seek a post.

Disasters used to befall citizens.
Gaping commoners in distress had yet to
    recover.
His directions brought peace and order to the
    land.
His cleaning efforts offered relief all over.

Recluses bowed at this place of ascension
    like Lake Ding.
At the mausoleum, officers and men were in
    sorrow.
In his jade burial robe, he ascended at dawn,
Leaving sweating funerary bronze horses,
    ever charging, never slow.

Under pine and cypress, I gaze at the empty
    halls.
Amid dust and sand, I stand on a dark
    pathway.
As I wander all over the mountain,
Alone and desolate, I think of the dynasty's
    founding day.

憶鄭南

鄭南伏毒寺，瀟灑到江心。石影銜珠閣，
泉聲帶玉琴。風杉曾曙倚，雲嶠憶春臨。
萬里滄浪外，龍蛇只自深。

Recalling South of Zheng

Fudu Temple, in south Zheng County,
Stands at mid-stream, with ease and grace.
The brook sounds like that of a jade zither.
The pearl-like pavilion and shadows of rocks
　　blend in the same space.
I once leaned on a wind-swept fir at dawn
And recalled spring's coming with clouds
　　at a high place.
Myriad miles away, beyond gray waves,
Hidden dragons and snakes do not surface.

喜雨

南國旱無雨，今朝江出雲。入空纔漠漠，
灑迴已紛紛。巢燕高飛盡，林花潤色分。
晚來聲不絕，應得夜深聞。

Rejoicing over the Rain

This morn, in the south lands long in drought,
Above the river, clouds came in sight.
Rain in sprays has spread all over,
With unmoving clouds first looking slight.
Moist forest blooms show unique colors.
All nestling swallows fly off at a height.
At twilight, the sound of rain does not stop.
I should be able to hear it late at night.

白水明府舅宅喜雨（得過字）

吾舅政如此， 古人誰復過。 碧山晴又溼，
白水雨徧多。 精禱既不昧， 歡娛將如何？
湯年旱頗甚， 今日醉弦歌。

Rejoicing over the Rain at the House of my Uncle, Magistrate of White Water County (My Allotted Word is "Outdone")

Such is the success of my uncle as the chief.
In history, it cannot be outdone.
At Whitewater, much rain is all over.
Green hills receive moisture under the sun.
His earnest prayers did not go unanswered.
How great will be our joy and fun!

King Tang had years of severe drought.
Today, unrestricted wine and song are for
everyone.

敬贈鄭諫議十韻

諫官非不達，詩義早知名。破的由來事，
先鋒孰敢爭。思飄雲物外，律中鬼神驚。
毫髮無遺恨，波瀾獨老成。野人寧得所，
天意薄浮生。多病休儒服，冥搜信客旌。
築居仙縹緲，旅食歲崢嶸　使者求顏闔，
諸公厭彌衡。將期一諾重，欻使寸心傾
君見窮途苦，宜憂阮步兵

Respectfully Presented to Remonstrator Zheng in Ten Couplets

The post of a remonstrator is no failure.
Early on, your poems have earned you fame.
Your messages are always to the point.
Except you, as a forerunner, who would dare
   fight to claim?

Your ideas fly beyond clouds and things.
Your poetic rhymes and tones give ghosts
   and spirits fright.

The turns and twists of your meters are
    singularly mature.
There is no lingering regret, however slight.

How can this rustic find his niche?
My drifting life is not favored by Heaven's
    will and manner.
Usually sick, I discard my scholar's robe.
In the dark void, I seek the worshippers'
    banner.

I shall build my dwelling by the fairies, far
    and dim.
In years as a wanderer, to loftiness my
    values have been attested.
Like Yan He, I was once sought by the king's
    messenger.
Like Mi Heng, by cliques of the court I was
    detested.

I would hope for your weighty promise
Which should quickly win over this heart
    of sincerity.
If you see one weeping at a roadblock in
    life,
Please send your concern for infantryman
    Ruan and me.

沙鷗：杜甫詩集

陳鈞洪譯

www.ingramcontent.com/pod-product-compliance
Lightning Source LLC
Chambersburg PA
CBHW051856090426

42811CB00003B/355